Securing Your Legacy
A Baby Boomer's Guide to Long Term Care Planning for Adult Children with Disabilities

Guild of Seven

Copyright © 2023 Guild of Seven

Celestar Publishing LLC

All rights reserved.

ISBN: 979-8-9873392-2-0

DEDICATION

Dedicated to the Baby Boomers,
whose unwavering commitment to their children with disabilities has inspired generations.

Parents of children with special needs in the Baby Boomer generation have shown unflinching love and compassion for their children. Their devotion to their children has changed the world for them, providing them with equal chances in school, health care, and every other area of life.

Their persistent work has pushed back against discriminatory practices and prepared the path for a more accepting culture. Their dedication to one another and their ability to persevere in the face of adversity have launched a movement that is changing attitudes, breaking down barriers, and bringing people together. Their kindness will live on to teach future generations of the transformative power of love and the infinite potential that lies inside each of us.

Disclaimer:

The information provided in this book is intended for informational purposes only and is not a substitute for professional advice. The author and publisher make no representations or warranties with respect to the accuracy, applicability, or completeness of the contents of this book. The information contained in this book is not intended as professional, financial, or medical advice, and should not be used as such.

Readers are strongly advised to seek professional guidance and consult with appropriate experts in the relevant fields when making decisions that may affect their personal, financial, or medical well-being. The content in this book is based on the knowledge and information available up to the publication date, which is current as of September 2021. As knowledge and circumstances change over time, readers are encouraged to verify the accuracy and applicability of the information to their specific situations.

The author and publisher shall not be held liable for any direct, indirect, incidental, consequential, or special damages arising out of or in any way connected with the use of the information in this book. It is the reader's responsibility to use their judgment and discretion when applying the content from this book to their own circumstances.

By reading this book, you acknowledge and agree to the terms of this disclaimer, and you accept full responsibility for any actions or decisions you make based on the information contained herein.

Contents

Dedication 3

Disclaimer: 4

Introduction 6

Finding Balance 9

Asking For Help 28

Securing Finances 45

Mental Wellness 61

When I Am Gone 69

How To Prepare For Unforeseen Circumstances While I'm Still Present .. 84

Planning The Conclusion Of My Affairs 94

Final Thouhgts 104

The Guild Of Seven 106

Acknowledgement 106

Bibliography 109

ONE

Introduction

Shall We Begin? But first...

Witnessing your children's weddings. Seeing them become parents themselves. Sharing precious moments with them as they embark on their own family journeys. These are the dreams and aspirations that many parents have as they approach their later years. However, for parents of children with disabilities, the path may look different.

The primary focus for many parents raising children with disabilities is ensuring their child's happiness and providing them with the best possible life. While this remains the ultimate goal, these parents often find themselves navigating unfamiliar territory as their children grow up and transition into adulthood.

The challenges become even more intricate when parents themselves are entering the twilight of their lives, grappling with concerns about their adult child's future. They may have experienced the loss of a spouse and may be facing their own health issues.

This book aims to serve as a guide for parents who find themselves in this situation. It seeks to reassure them that they are not alone and to share the stories of other parents who have walked a similar path. Moreover, it endeavors to help them embark on a journey of securing the well-being of their child even after they, the parents, have passed away, and to witness the fruits of their efforts while they are still alive.

However, before we delve into the contents of this book, let's take a moment to acquaint ourselves with each other. Who are we, and why did we write this book?

The Guild of Seven was driven to create this resource because we understand the concerns that weigh heavily on your minds. The well-being and happiness of your adult children is your utmost priority, and ensuring they receive the best possible care is a responsibility that can sometimes feel overwhelming. We want you to know that you are not alone in this journey.

We believe that every individual deserves to live a life of dignity, respect, and fulfillment, regardless of their abilities. We know that you share this belief wholeheartedly, and it is this shared commitment that has motivated us to compile this guide.

The purpose of this guide is to empower you, to provide you with knowledge, insights, and practical advice that will assist you in making informed decisions about long-term care for your adult children with disabilities. We want to help alleviate the anxiety and uncertainty that often accompany such decisions and guide you towards finding the most suitable care options that will enhance their quality of life.

Through this guide, we aim to address various aspects of long-term care, including navigating healthcare systems, understanding legal considerations, finding supportive communities, and accessing appropriate services and resources. We have meticulously gathered information from experts in the field, consulted with caregivers and families who have firsthand experience, and conducted extensive research to ensure the guide is comprehensive and reliable.

We want to emphasize that the intention behind this guide is not to dictate what is best for your adult children, as every individual is unique and requires personalized care. Instead, our goal is to equip you with the knowledge and resources necessary to make well-informed decisions that align with your loved one's specific needs, preferences, and aspirations.

By sharing our collective wisdom, experiences, and insights, we hope to ease your burden and empower you to navigate the intricate maze of long-term care confidently. We firmly believe that with the right support and information, you can continue to provide the loving and nurturing environment that your adult children with disabilities deserve.

Please remember, dear Boomers, that you are incredible advocates and caregivers. Your commitment to your adult children's well-being is a testament to your love and strength. We stand by your side, offering our support and encouragement as you embark on this journey. Together, let us ensure that your adult children lead lives that are rich with opportunities, happiness, and fulfillment.

As professionals, we've been fortunate to have the invaluable opportunity to meet and collaborate with numerous families who have children with disabilities. Throughout our journey, we have witnessed both the joys and sorrows, the triumphs and defeats experienced by these families. Their stories have been shared with us, and we have actively engaged in their aspirations fortheir children.

Furthermore, we have observed the challenges faced by many parents as their children mature and transition into adulthood. Concerns about the future well-being of their children when they are no longer able to provide care weigh heavily on their minds. However, it is important to recognize that worry alone is not the greatest obstacle. Helplessness is the true enemy.

Worry only consumes us if we allow it to do so. By taking action and proactively addressing the concerns, worry can become a helpful ally. Conversely, helplessness acts like a slow but relentless cancer, eroding our spirit and resolve.

In this book, our mission is to combat this malignancy of helplessness. Drawing from our expertise and experience, we will provide practical advice and share stories from other parents, aiming to impart valuable lessons. We invite you, as a parent of an adult child with a disability, to join us on this journey. Along the way, we will explore ways for you to care for both yourself and your child in the present, while also developing concrete plans for their future encompassing various aspects such as finances, education/work, relationships, and more.

We assure you that the journey will be worthwhile, offering numerous insights and knowledge. Ladies and gentlemen, shall we embark on this transformative path together?

TWO

FINDING BALANCE

How can I balance caring for someone while also taking care of myself?

Navigating the complexities of caregiving can be incredibly demanding, especially when faced with the need for personal care in the future. In an era that often prioritizes individual desires and needs, grasping the significance of self-care can pose a challenge, particularly when caring for a loved one.

However, it is vital to recognize that taking the time and effort to recharge one's own batteries plays a pivotal role in providing the best possible care for others. As parents of children with disabilities, the concern of how to care for ourselves when we eventually require it is a question that many baby-boomer elderly parents confront, and one that does not always have a straightforward answer.

Within this chapter, we aim to shed light on the importance of self-care, offering valuable insights and practical tips to help you prioritize your well-being. Additionally, we will direct your attention to alternative ways you can provide care and support for your child, thus alleviating some of the anxieties that come with balancing personal care and caregiving responsibilities.

By the conclusion of this chapter, you will gain a deeper understanding of how to effectively care for both yourself and your loved one, establishing a harmonious equilibrium that promotes overall well-being.

Let us embark on this journey together, discovering the significance of self-care while navigating the path of caring for those we hold dear.

Do I require care for myself?

A member of The Guild had a nostalgic memory of her first airplane trip as a teenager, accompanied by her mother. She struggled to comprehend the workings of the aircraft and relied on her mother's assistance to understand how the seat belts operated. She distinctly recalls chuckling when the cabin crew advised that in the event of an emergency, passengers with young children should secure their own oxygen masks first before assisting others.

Initially, she found this advice to be selfish. How could one prioritize their own oxygen mask when their child needed it? However, as she has grown older, she has come to realize that putting on your own oxygen mask first is not selfish at all—it's a wise decision.

You see, in order to care for another person, it is essential to care for yourself first. Consider the scenario on an airplane: if the oxygen masks drop down and you attempt to help your child put on their mask before securing yours, you are likely to pass out from lack of oxygen and become unable to assist them. The same principle applies when caring for a disabled child.

Caring for someone else can be straightforward on certain days but more challenging on others. When other aspects of life demand our attention and focus, such as long work hours, travel, or personal difficulties like health issues or anxiety, it can be difficult for us to maintain our usual cheerful and positive demeanor while providing care for our children.

This is why parents must recognize their responsibility to themselves as the primary pillars of support for their disabled child. It is not sustainable to continuously operate on empty without taking breaks, as it may lead to burnout. Parents of disabled children need to be capable of providing physical, emotional, and mental care on multiple levels.

It is only natural for parents to prioritize their child's needs above their own, but it is important to acknowledge that continuous neglect of self-care can lead to exhaustion. To effectively care for their disabled children, parents must also prioritize their own well-being. By dedicating time to self-care, parents can mitigate feelings of being overwhelmed, cultivate patience, and be fully present for their children. This, in turn, allows them to provide care for their child in a more efficient and effective manner.

Furthermore, parents who make self-care a priority are imparting a valuable lesson to their children—the significance of taking care of oneself. By modeling self-care behaviors, parents are teaching their children essential skills that will serve them well throughout their lives. They are demonstrating the importance of nurturing their own physical, mental, and emotional well-being, thus equipping them with the tools to navigate challenges and maintain a balanced and healthy lifestyle.

By recognizing the vital role that self-care plays in caregiving, parents can create a positive ripple effect that extends beyond their immediate relationship with their disabled children. They are not only enhancing their own well-being but also fostering a culture of self-care and resilience within their family, empowering their children to prioritize their own needs and nurturing their overall development.

Therefore, by valuing self-care, parents can rejuvenate themselves, enhance their caregiving abilities, and instill in their children the lifelong importance of caring for oneself. It is a transformative approach that fosters a harmonious balance between the well-being of both parents and children, ensuring a healthier and more fulfilling journey together.

What type of care do you need as a parent of an adult child with a disability?

As a parent of an adult child with a disability, you require care on various fronts—physical, emotional, and mental.

Physical Care:

Taking care of your physical well-being is crucial, as it enables you to have the energy and vitality necessary to provide optimal care for your child. Here are some strategies to prioritize your physical health:

1. Rest and Sleep: Make sure you prioritize sufficient rest and quality sleep. Adequate rest allows your body to recharge and rejuvenate, enabling you to tackle your caregiving responsibilities with renewed energy.

2. Nutritious Meals: Despite the time constraints, aim to consume balanced and nutritious meals. Opt for fresh fruits, vegetables, whole grains, lean proteins, and healthy fats. Planning and preparing meals in advance or exploring meal delivery services can help streamline the process.

3. Exercise: Incorporate physical activity into your daily routine, even if you have limited time. During your child's rest periods, take a quick walk around the neighborhood, or engage in simple exercises at home. On weekends, explore accessible areas where you can enjoy outdoor activities with your child. Regular exercise not only benefits your physical health but also enhances your mental well-being.

4. Mobility Challenges: As you age, mobility challenges may arise. Conditions like arthritis, joint pain, or muscle weakness can make movement difficult. Explore mobility aids such as walkers, canes, or scooters to enhance your mobility and maintain an active lifestyle. Volunteer transportation services and paratransit options can also aid with reaching appointments and running errands.

5. Domestic Tasks: As you transition into retirement and age, domestic tasks may become more challenging. Seek assistance from relatives, non-disabled siblings, or domestic workers to handle tasks like cooking, cleaning, and gardening. Additionally, consider adopting smart home devices that can automate certain activities, such as monitoring your child's movement, managing medication, or controlling household appliances. These devices reduce your physical burden and give you more time for self-care.

6. Home-Based Services: Explore the possibility of receiving home-based healthcare services. Telemedicine platforms allow you to consult with doctors and healthcare professionals from the comfort of your home, saving you travel time and costs. Furthermore, consider home visits from doctors or specialized healthcare providers to minimize the physical exertion of traveling to medical appointments.

7. Geriatric Wellness Programs: Engage in low-cost geriatric wellness programs that focus on healthy aging and preventing chronic diseases. These programs often provide health education, screenings, vaccinations, counseling, and exercise classes tailored to older adults. Participating in these programs can enhance your physical well-being and provide valuable support and guidance.

Prioritizing your physical care is not selfish—it is an essential component of being an effective caregiver. By taking care of yourself, you ensure that you have the stamina and vitality needed to provide the best care for your child with disabilities.

Well-Being

In addition to the previous points, ensuring proper nutrition is a vital aspect of maintaining your physical well-being. Consuming healthy meals that provide essential nutrients is key to sustaining your energy levels and overall health. Consider consulting with a nutrition counselor who can assess your specific dietary needs and provide personalized guidance. Online nutrition counseling services such as Lemond Nutrition, Anderson's Nutrition, and Amwell offer convenient access to professional advice in this area.

Regular check-ups and screenings with your doctor are crucial for monitoring your health and detecting any potential issues at an early stage. By staying proactive about your health, you can address concerns promptly and receive appropriate treatment when needed. These routine appointments help you stay on top of your well-being, providing you with the energy and resilience necessary to care for your child.

Taking care of your physical health is not only beneficial for yourself but also for your ability to provide dedicated care to your child with disabilities. Prioritizing self-care and paying attention to your own needs ensures that you have the physical strength and vitality to fulfill your caregiving responsibilities effectively. By taking proactive steps to maintain your well-being, you can approach your role as a caregiver with renewed energy and be better equipped to support your child's needs.

Emotional Care

Caring for your emotional well-being is just as important as attending to your physical needs. Taking practical steps to calm down and effectively manage your emotions are vital aspects of emotional self-care. It is crucial to find healthy outlets to express your feelings, as bottling them up can lead to unhealthy manifestations. By taking proactive steps to relax, manage your emotions, and seek support, when necessary, you can greatly enhance your overall emotional health. Here are some strategies to prioritize emotional self-care:

1. Communication and Support: Share your feelings and experiences with your spouse or partner, as they can provide valuable support and understanding. If you're a surviving partner, confiding in a close friend or relative can also be helpful. Opening up and discussing your emotions with trusted individuals can provide a sense of relief and reassurance.

2. Writing and Support Groups: Some parents find solace in writing in a diary or journal, expressing their thoughts and emotions freely. Participating in parent support groups or online forums can also provide a safe space for sharing experiences, gaining insights, and connecting with others who may be facing similar challenges.

3. Counseling and Therapy: Regular sessions with a counselor or therapist can offer significant emotional support. Although scheduling appointments might be challenging, there are remote counseling options available. Explore telemedicine service providers that offer emotional counseling. Apps and platforms such as Better Help, Faithful Counseling, Calmerry, Calm, Shine, Moodnotes, Wysa, Woebot, and MARCo provide convenient access to professional counselors who can provide the guidance and support you need.

4. Emotional Connection with Your Child: Cultivate open and honest communication with your child. Share your emotions, both positive and negative, with them. Express gratitude for their presence in your life and celebrate their accomplishments. Acknowledge their impact and how they have helped you grow as a person. During challenging times, reassure them of your love and appreciation, fostering a deep emotional bond. Children with disabilities often have a keen understanding of their parents' vulnerabilities and are eager to provide support in their own unique ways. Simply being present and listening attentively can be incredibly meaningful and nurturing for both parent and child.

By prioritizing your emotional care, you can cultivate patience, resilience, and a stronger connection with your child. Taking the time to understand and express your emotions allows for a deeper understanding of yourself and your child, fostering a meaningful and supportive relationship. Remember, you don't have to face emotional challenges alone—seeking support and nurturing emotional connections can greatly contribute to your overall well-being as a caregiver.

Mental Care

Arranging breaks from caregiving, nurturing relationships with friends and family, and engaging in activities that bring you joy are all crucial aspects of maintaining good mental health.

It is essential to carve out time for yourself and pursue activities that you enjoy during your free time, allowing you to maintain a life beyond the caregiver role. Whether it's reading a book, taking a dance class, or meeting a friend for coffee, find activities that bring you happiness and invest more energy into doing them.

If you appreciate community involvement, consider joining a local or online book club or participating in free or affordable online cooking classes from platforms like Cozymeal, Home Made Cooking, Delia Online Cookery School, and others.

Some churches also offer spiritual and mental health support units for members who may be facing mental challenges. Additionally, there are Facebook support groups such as Anxiety Lounge, Anxiety and Depression Support Group, Mental Health America, Mental Health Awareness and Support, and more that can provide a supportive community.

For virtual mental health support, you can explore free mobile applications developed by real-life psychologists like Chatowl, Elomia, Youper, and others. Alternatively, volunteer online therapy platforms like 7 Cups, Bliss, and professional therapy sites like Ginger, which partner with employers, insurers, and health providers, offer human alternatives.

It's important to recognize that experiencing mental health issues, such as anxiety, depression, or other mental illnesses, is not uncommon among baby boomers. Research conducted by the CDC in 2013 revealed that about 25% of adults aged 65 years or older have some form of mental health problem, including mood disorders not associated with normal aging.

Furthermore, according to a 2018 survey by the American Psychiatric Association on anxiety levels among different generations, baby boomers experienced the most significant increase in anxiety, with a seven-point jump within a year.

By taking care of your mental health, including seeking support when needed and engaging in activities that bring you happiness, you can better navigate the challenges of caregiving and enhance your overall well-being.

According to a study conducted in 2020, it is projected that the rates of dementia among baby boomers born between 1948 and 1959 will surpass those of previous generations due to a higher prevalence of cognitive decline within this demographic.

In light of this, it is important to not only engage in activities that provide mental relaxation and recreation but also consider seeking professional assistance and counseling for any cognitive difficulties that may arise as you age.

Depression & Mental Well-Being

If you are experiencing symptoms associated with depression or dementia-related disorders, putting your mental well-being first becomes even more crucial. Taking proactive steps to maintain your mental health is essential, regardless of your current cognitive abilities. Here are some recommendations to consider:

1. Stay mentally active and engaged: Engaging in intellectually stimulating activities, such as joining a book club or taking a cooking class, helps keep your mind sharp and reduces cognitive decline.

2. Engage in physical exercise: Regular exercise not only improves mental health and brain function but also helps reduce stress levels, which can significantly contribute to cognitive decline.

3. Control high blood pressure: High blood pressure is recognized as a risk factor for dementia. It is important to have it regularly checked and take steps to keep it under control.

4. Explore intervention treatments: If you are at risk of dementia, various intervention treatments can be considered, including smoking cessation, diabetes management, hormone therapy, depression treatment, and cholesterol-reducing therapies.

5. Cognitive Rehabilitation Therapy: For those already experiencing cognitive decline, Cognitive Rehabilitation Therapy offers rehabilitative care. Writing activities and engagement with computer-assisted programs can help improve memory, attention processing, social communication, problem-solving skills, and emotional regulation.

6. Implement supportive measures: Smart home assistants, like Alexa or Google Assistants, can provide reminders for medication, doctor's appointments, and daily tasks. Motion sensor-equipped smart lighting can assist with navigation in your home.

7. Carve out "me-time": Even with limited free time, it is important to find moments for yourself. Consider setting your alarm earlier in the morning or arranging for your spouse or partner to watch your child for an hour so you can engage in activities that bring you joy.

8. Explore caregiver options: Hiring a caregiver to live with you or hiring respite carers who assist during specific times can provide valuable support. Ensure compliance with legal requirements and consider hosting a volunteer caregiver in exchange for room and board.

9. Seek assistance from relatives: If possible, involve relatives in caregiving. Explore programs that provide payment to family caregivers, such as the Home and Community-Based Services (HCBS) Program, Medicaid, and the Personal Care Attendant Program.

10. Enroll in Rehabilitation Services: Consider enrolling your child in Rehabilitation Services, which can assist with their development in cognitive, physical, speech, and emotional domains. These services can also provide accessibility equipment to support their employability.

By taking these steps, you can prioritize your mental well-being and ensure that you have the support and resources necessary to navigate the challenges of caregiving while maintaining your own health and happiness. By now, you are likely already well-versed in the medical care your disabled child requires and how to attend to their physical needs. However, caring for a disabled child extends beyond meeting their basic necessities and assisting with daily tasks they are unable to perform independently. Just like any individual, your children require more than just physical and medical care to ensure their overall well-being.

Understanding the specific type of care your disabled child needs can be challenging, especially as they transition into adulthood. It was perhaps easier when they were younger and their needs primarily revolved around tangible tasks such as school assignments, medication management, and doctor visits. However, as they grow older, their needs will evolve, necessitating changes in your caregiving approach.

Here are some examples of the types of care your adult child with a disability may require as they enter different stages of life:

1. Providing a Calm and Supportive Environment: Each child with a disability has unique preferences, and there is no one-size-fits-all approach to creating the ideal environment for them. Some children thrive in highly structured settings, while others may prefer a more relaxed atmosphere. As their parent, you possess intimate knowledge of your child's personality and preferences, allowing you to determine the environment that suits them best.

It is crucial to establish a calm and supportive environment for your child, considering that raising a child with disabilities can be stressful at times. This may involve setting aside dedicated time each day to have meaningful conversations or involving them in family activities, even if they can only participate to a limited extent. Providing structure and routine, while remaining flexible and responsive to their needs, can contribute to a supportive environment. It is beneficial to set reasonable expectations, establish clear rules, and be open to listening to your child's perspective.

Additionally, facilitating opportunities for your adult child to socialize and interact with peers is essential for their development. Creating a physically and emotionally safe environment further contributes to their overall well-being.

2. Emotional Support: Beyond physical care, your child requires emotional support as they navigate the challenges associated with their disability. This support involves being empathetic, understanding, and validating their feelings and experiences. Encouraging open communication and actively listening to their concerns can foster a strong emotional connection. Your presence and unwavering support can make a significant difference in their lives.

3. Advocacy and Empowerment: As your child grows older, it becomes crucial to empower them to advocate for themselves and make decisions to the best of their abilities. Encouraging self-advocacy skills can foster independence and confidence. Teach them about their rights, available resources, and how to communicate their needs effectively. Empowering your child in this way prepares them to navigate the challenges they may encounter in various aspects of their life.

4. Continued Learning and Skill Development: Supporting your adult child's ongoing learning and skill development is essential. This can involve exploring educational opportunities tailored to their needs, such as special education programs, vocational training, or inclusive learning environments. Encouraging their interests and hobbies can contribute to their personal growth and provide them with a sense of purpose and fulfillment.

5. Future Planning: As your child approaches adulthood, it is important to engage in future planning discussions. This includes considering their long-term care, financial stability, and guardianship arrangements. Exploring options such as setting up a trust, accessing government benefits, and identifying suitable housing options can provide peace of mind and ensure your child's well-being in the future.

Consider that every child with a disability is unique, and their care needs will vary. By continually assessing their needs, communicating with professionals, and seeking support from relevant organizations, you can ensure that your child receives the comprehensive care they deserve.

Encouraging Independence

Recognizing that your child with a disability is now an adult who desires independence and privacy is an important aspect of caring for them. While they may still rely on you for certain things, it is crucial to support their journey towards autonomy in areas unaffected by their condition. Consider these techniques to promote their independence:

1. Grant freedom of choice: Allow your adult child with autism, for example, to make decisions regarding their clothing preferences, as long as it does not compromise their safety.

2. Reduce supervision gradually: If your child can manage their grooming, consider decreasing the level of supervision you provide for their daily personal care. However, periodically inquire about their personal care to determine if any assistance is needed.

3. Facilitate access to adaptive equipment: Help your child find adaptive equipment or devices that enable them to perform tasks independently. Adaptive equipment does not have to be extravagant or expensive; it can be as simple as a cup with a straw for someone with grip difficulties or a long-handled loofah for easier bathing.

4. Explore adaptive tools: Introduce specially designed utensils, wheelchairs, or computer software that assist individuals with disabilities in living more independently.

Encouraging independence not only makes your life easier but also enhances your child's sense of capability and competence. It aids in their cognitive development by fostering problem-solving and critical thinking skills. Furthermore, promoting independence contributes to their emotional growth, resilience in challenging situations, and boosts self-esteem and self-confidence.

Involvement in Tasks

Another way to care for your disabled child is by involving them in various tasks. This can include household chores like setting the table or folding laundry. Moreover, taking them along on errands such as grocery shopping or visiting the post office can be beneficial.

Involving your child in tasks not only helps them feel useful and needed but also enables them to acquire new skills. For example, participating in meal preparation can teach them how to cook simple meals. Tailor the tasks based on their disability type and interests, ensuring they are both appropriate and engaging.

Respect as an Adult and Open Communication

One of the most meaningful ways to show care for your disabled child is to acknowledge their adulthood and treat them accordingly. Foster open communication by sharing your thoughts, feelings, and concerns while actively listening to theirs. Be honest and transparent about various aspects, even if they may be challenging to discuss.

For instance, if you are facing financial difficulties, be open about it, explaining the situation and its potential impact. Involve them in finding solutions and working together as a team. Communicating openly demonstrates that you value and respect them as adults, building trust and making difficult conversations easier in the long run.

By encouraging independence, involving them in tasks, and respecting their adulthood through open communication, you provide comprehensive care for your disabled child, fostering their growth, self-reliance, and mutual understanding.

Help Them Learn Skills That Can Keep Them Engaged and Support Their Livelihood

While discussing difficult topics, it is important to address the inevitable reality of your passing. For parents of adults with disabilities whose intellectual development is not severely affected, one way to care for your child beyond your lifetime is by helping them acquire skills that are practical, engaging, and enable them to earn a living.

Enrolling your child in training programs that teach essential workplace skills is a valuable approach. For instance, programs like the Oireachtas Work Learning (OWL) program provide real-world learning experiences that prepare individuals for work and increase their chances of securing employment opportunities.

Parents can actively support their children's intellectual and economic needs by teaching them skills necessary for independent work. It is also crucial to identify specific skills required for particular job roles. Seeking assistance from a rehabilitation counselor can be beneficial in this regard. These professionals assess your child's abilities, identify potential job opportunities, provide adaptive devices, and teach them how to effectively use these tools in the workplace. Ongoing counseling services should be arranged to ensure continuity of support in the event of your absence or inability to care for your child.

Another approach is to familiarize your child with the realities of modern remote work. The traditional 9-5 office culture is rapidly changing, with remote-friendly job opportunities on the rise. This shift presents an opportunity to support your child by helping them engage in meaningful work.

Regardless of disability, certain key skills are essential for modern workers. Effective online communication skills, including email, instant messaging, and video conferencing, are crucial. Proficiency in productivity tools like Google Docs or Microsoft Office is important, as is the ability to work independently and manage time effectively.

If your adult child with a disability is interested in pursuing remote work, you can take steps to assist them. Introduce them to remote work concepts and explain how it functions. Help them identify the skills necessary for remote employment. Once their skill set has been evaluated, teach them the fundamentals of working remotely. Support them in creating a dedicated workspace at home and guide them through the process of applying for remote jobs. Provide ongoing support as they transition into their career. With your assistance, your disabled adult child can thrive in the working world, achieving full independence and autonomy.

By helping your child acquire relevant skills, explore remote work opportunities, and actively supporting their career development, you demonstrate your unwavering commitment to their well-being. Your efforts ensure they have the tools and opportunities to lead fulfilling lives even in your absence, reflecting the tremendous care and love you have devoted to their journey.

Preparing Them for Your Passing and Supporting Their Transition

The loss of a parent is an incredibly challenging experience, and for adults with disabilities, this can be even more daunting. While there is no universal solution to navigating grief, there are steps that elderly parents can take to help their children cope better when they pass away.

First and foremost, it is crucial to engage in open and honest conversations about grief and loss. By having these discussions, you can help normalize the emotions associated with death and prepare your children for the inevitable reality of your passing. These conversations provide an opportunity to express feelings, share memories, and create a safe space for processing emotions.

In addition, it is important to have frank conversations about what to expect after your death. Addressing topics such as changes in routines, living arrangements, and support systems can help alleviate some of the fear and uncertainty that often accompany grief. By openly discussing these matters, you provide your children with a sense of preparedness and enable them to face the future with greater resilience.

A Difficult Conversation

Having a compassionate talk with your adult child about your eventual death and passing on can be a difficult but important conversation, especially when your child has a disability. It's natural to feel a range of emotions and concerns while discussing such a sensitive topic, but approaching it with empathy, honesty, and support can help ease the process. Here are some guidelines to help you have a compassionate conversation with your adult child with a disability:

1. Choose the right time and place: Find a comfortable and quiet setting where you can have an uninterrupted conversation. Make sure both of you have enough time to discuss the topic thoroughly without feeling rushed or overwhelmed.

2. Prepare yourself emotionally: It's essential to acknowledge and process your own emotions surrounding your mortality before having this conversation. Take the time to reflect on your feelings, fears, and hopes. This will help you approach the discussion with more clarity and composure.

3. Be honest and transparent: While it might be tempting to shield your child from the idea of your passing, it's important to be honest about the realities of life and death. Use simple and clear language to explain that death is a natural part of life and that it happens to everyone, including yourself. Emphasize that this conversation is a way for both of you to be prepared and ensure their well-being in the future.

4. Validate their emotions: Your child may experience a range of emotions when discussing your eventual passing. It's crucial to create a safe space where they can express their fears, concerns, and sadness. Let them know that their emotions are valid and understandable and reassure them that you are there to support them throughout the process.

5. Discuss future plans and arrangements: Talk about your wishes and any plans you have made for their future care and support. This may include financial matters, legal documents such as wills and power of attorney, and arrangements for their living situation. Involve them in decision-making as much as possible, giving them a sense of autonomy and control.

6. Reassure them of ongoing support: One of the biggest concerns your child may have is the loss of your support and presence. Reassure them that you are taking steps to ensure they will continue to receive the care they need even after you are gone. Discuss any support networks, family members, or organizations that can provide assistance and reassurance in the future.

7. Provide written documentation: Consider preparing written documentation, such as a letter or a document outlining your wishes and plans. This can serve as a reference point and offer them a sense of security and clarity when the time comes.

8. Seek professional guidance if needed: If you feel overwhelmed or unsure about how to approach this conversation, consider seeking guidance from professionals such as therapists, social workers, or support groups. They can provide valuable insights and help you navigate through the emotional challenges associated with discussing end-of-life matters.

Truly, this conversation is an ongoing process, and it may take time for your child to fully grasp and come to terms with the idea. Be patient, open to their questions, and continue to offer support and reassurance. By having a compassionate and honest conversation, you can help your adult child with a disability feel more prepared and supported for the future.

Fostering Independence

Encouraging your child to develop independence, as mentioned earlier, remains a crucial aspect of their preparation. Empowering them to acquire life skills, make decisions, and navigate daily challenges enhances their self-confidence and ability to adapt to life without you. By fostering their independence, you equip them with the tools they need to lead fulfilling lives.

Moreover, it is vital to assist your children in making legal and financial arrangements for their future well-being. If your child is unable to make adult choices, it may be necessary to establish pre-arranged processes with the court to appoint a guardian who can advocate for their interests after your passing or if you are unable to fulfill this role during your lifetime.

Financial planning is also paramount. Some public services have asset limitations, such as the requirement to have less than $2,000 in assets to qualify for SSI. Inheriting assets or being designated as a life insurance policy beneficiary could inadvertently disqualify your child from receiving essential benefits. To safeguard their eligibility, setting up a special needs trust can preserve your child's inheritance while ensuring they continue to receive government support. Another valuable financial tool is an ABLE Account, which is a tax-advantaged savings account allowing your disabled child to accumulate up to $100,000 without jeopardizing government subsidies.

Addressing your child's specific needs, such as housing, is also crucial. If you wish for your child to reside in a group home after your passing, it is vital to initiate the registration process as soon as possible. This ensures they are placed on the waiting list and secures their position in the facility, providing them with stability and support.

Finally, establishing a support group consisting of individuals who are willing to be present in your child's life and whom they feel comfortable having in theirs can greatly assist their transition. This group can offer emotional and practical support, aid with day-to-day tasks, act as a sounding board for decision-making, and provide valuable feedback throughout the transition process. By carefully selecting group members and involving your child in the process, you help them create a supportive network that will be invaluable during this period of change.

While it is impossible to eliminate the pain of loss, taking these steps can help ease the transition for adults with disabilities. By addressing legal, financial, and practical considerations and fostering a supportive environment, you empower your children to face the future with strength and resilience.

Resource Hub:

Mobility Aids

Organization Name	Contact Info (Aid/Application Page)	Location	Special Note
American Outreach Foundation	https://www.americanoutreachfoundation.com (https://www.americanoutreachfoundation.com/copy-of-donatea-powerchair) (760) 673-7982 NeedAPowerchair@Yahoo.com	Coachella Valley, California, USA.	1. This service is currently restricted to Coachella Valley 2. You may not qualify for this service if the foundation finds that: • It is against your doctor's advice • You can afford to get the mobility aids yourself • You are qualified to get such aid from your insurance provider
Hope Haven	http://hopehaveninernational.org/ (https://www.hopehaven.org/media/files/2021%20Wheelchair%20Application0Form%20%20Fillable%20PDF%20%20Copy%201.pdf) (712) 476-2737	Rock Valley, Sioux, Iowa, USA	1. This service is not restricted by location. Therefore, you can contact them from anywhere in the world. 2. Hope Haven also offers spiritual support, mental health & recovery, day habilitation, employment services, and community living services.
Friends of Disabled Adults and Children	https://fodac.org/ (https://fodac.org/medical-equipment/) (770) 491-9014	Atlanta, Georgia, USA	1. This organization serves only those within the state of Georgia. 2. FODAC also helps with other assistive tech devices and can make vehicle modifications for a small fee.
The Kids Equipment Network	https://tken.org/ (https://tken.org/access-equipment/)	Chicago USA	1. Although this organization only serves the needs of children in Chicago, they actively recommend reaching out to them for device assistance. Even if their service does not extend to your location, they will try to link you up with a local organization closer to you
Independence At Home	http://www.independenceathome.org.uk/ (http://www.independenceathome.org.uk/how-to-apply.html) https://www.facebook.com/Independenceat-Home1081637025282220/ https://twitter.com/iahgrants (020) 8427- 7929	England and Wales, UK	1. All applications must be submitted on behalf of the individual by Referrers. See the How to Apply Page for a list of eligible referrers

Transportation Aid

Organization	Contact	Location	Special Note
Eldercare Locator	https://eldercare.acl.gov/Public/Resources/LearnMoreAbout/Transportation.aspx 1-800-677-1116	USA	1. The Eldercare Locator can help you learn about and connect with local transportation services anywhere in the USA
National Aging and Disability Transportation Center (NADTC)	https://www.nadtc.org/ 866-983-3222 contact@nadtc.org	USA	Community transportation options are often creative solutions meant to fill identified gaps. *Dial-a-ride which offers curb-to-curb service at an agreed-upon time. *Volunteer transportation programs; and *Assisted transportation ("door-to-door")
Easterseals	https://www.easterseals.com/programsandservices/transportation.html 800-221-6827	Chicago, Illinois USA	1.This organization helps you connect with local mobility managers that can help you get around. 2. They have a partnership with Travel For All, an organization that caters to the needs of disabled travelers and their caregivers.
Age UK	https://www.ageuk.org.uk/services/in-your-area/transport/ 0800 678 1602	London, England UK	Age UK works alongside other community organizations to provide door-to-door transport for older people UK-wide.
Royal Voluntary Services	https://www.royalvoluntaryservice.org.uk/our-services/getting-out-about/ 0330 555 0310	Cardiff, Wales UK	RVS services are available UK wide, and they provide both community and patient transport services.

Food Resources

Organization	Contact	Location	Special Note
Meals on Wheels, America	https://www.mealsonwheelsamerica.org/find-meals 1-888-998-6325	Virginia, USA	1. Meals on Wheels operates in every community in America through their network of more than 5,000 independently run local programs. 2. Depending on individual circumstances, meals may be provided along a sliding fee scale, from no cost to full price.
Feeding America	https://www.feedingamerica.org/find-yourlocal-foodbank 1-800-771-2303	Chicago, Illinois USA	1. This organization runs several food banks across the USA and helps individuals apply for national food programs.
Royal Voluntary Service	https://www.royalvoluntaryservice.org.uk/ 0845 608 0122	Cardiff, Wales UK	1. Royal Voluntary Service provides food delivery services on behalf of many local councils in the UK. 2. The driver will not only bring the meal to the home, but they also visit the older person or to ensure they are safe and secure.
Malnutrition Task Force	https://www.malnutritiontaskforce.org.uk/ 07769 363 429	London, England UK	1. This organization does not particularly give food grants or run food programs. Nonetheless, they provide helpful information that can help you determine what type of food is best for you.
Apetito	https://www.apetito.co.uk/ourservice/meals-on-wheels 01225 637054	Trowbridge, England UK	1.This organization also works with local authorities to deliver meals at low cost to people with a disability or older residents. 2. The Meals on Wheels drivers from Apetito will also provide other support to the vulnerable, such as checking on their health. 3. They also provide other initiatives aimed at helping the poor and vulnerable

Three

ASKING FOR HELP

At what point should I contemplate seeking assistance, and how can I go about finding it?

"Ari?" My father's voice was soft. "Ari, Ari, Ari. You're fighting this war in the worst possible way."

"I don't know how to fight it, Dad."

"You should ask for help," he said.

"I don't know how to do that, either."

(Benjamin Alire Sáenz in Aristotle and Dante Discover the Secrets of the Universe)

Let's explore the familiar situation further:

Ari's story serves as a reminder of the challenges parents face in providing the best care for their disabled children. Unlike Ari's immediate need for physical defense, parents often find themselves in a prolonged battle to ensure their children's well-being and success. However, there comes a point when they realize that seeking assistance is necessary, just as Ari did. Yet, like Ari, many parents are unsure of how to go about it.

     Asking for help is not always a straightforward task. It can be challenging and may require us to step outside our comfort zones. There is no need to downplay the difficulty of reaching out for support. However, if we genuinely want to provide the best possible care for our children, we must gather our courage and take the necessary steps.

Recognizing the need for help is a sign of strength, not weakness. It demonstrates our willingness to confront challenges head-on and actively seek the assistance required to overcome them. Therefore, do not hesitate to ask for help when the need arises. It may take courage, but reaching out can make a world of difference during difficult times.

It's important to remember that as time goes on, asking for help becomes easier. Through experience and practice, we become more comfortable with seeking support and recognizing that it is a vital part of providing optimal care for our children. So, with each step, the process of asking for help becomes more familiar and manageable.

Exploring the concept of the point of no return further:

Determining the point of no return is not an exact science, as it varies depending on the specific circumstances. However, one general guideline is when parents find themselves unable to provide the level of care their child needs. This can occur due to various factors, such as the child's increasing dependence or the declining health of the parent.

Assessing the point of no return involves considering multiple factors, including financial considerations, the parent's and child's medical conditions, the well-being of the caregiver, and more. For example, if tasks that were previously manageable for the parent, such as lifting heavy groceries or providing physical support, become too challenging due to the parent's diminishing strength, then the point of no return has likely been reached.

Another instance where external assistance may be necessary is the loss of one of the parents who were caring for the child. Trying to fulfill the roles of two parents alone can quickly become physically overwhelming for the surviving parent, leading to avoidable complications.

It's important to note that the point of no return is not solely determined by physical factors. Emotional exhaustion and the need for a break, such as grieving the loss of a loved one, adjusting to senior citizenship, or adapting to a new environment after relocation, can also signal the need for external help in providing the best care for the disabled child.

A sudden decline or deterioration in the cognitive abilities of the caregiving parent is another point of no return, as it can jeopardize the safety of both the parents and the child. Additionally, changes in the child's condition, such as increased dependency levels, may surpass the parents' capacity to provide the required level of care. [1]

Other examples of reaching the point of no return include when the child's medical condition necessitates round-the-clock care beyond the parents' capabilities or when the child's behavior becomes aggressive and challenging to manage. In such situations, it becomes increasingly difficult, if not impossible, for the parents to meet their child's needs adequately.

Often, the signs of reaching the point of no return become evident to those around the parent and even to the parent themselves. Ignoring these signs and continuing as usual would be unwise. It is better to face reality and seek assistance sooner rather than later to prevent further deterioration.

Regardless of the reason for seeking help, it is crucial not to wait until a crisis occurs before taking action. Planning and implementing measures to prevent reaching a tipping point is preferable. However, if a crisis does occur, being prepared and having a clear plan in place is essential.

When seeking assistance, it is important to have a clear understanding of the specific help needed and where to find it. Researching and planning for potential future needs, even if assistance is not immediately required, is advisable.

Recognizing that the point of no return has been reached is a difficult realization that is often accompanied by a heavy heart. However, it is important to remember that reaching this point does not mean the love between a parent and child has diminished. It simply indicates that the parent can no longer provide the necessary level of care.

It is also crucial to understand that seeking assistance does not equate to giving up control or responsibility. Instead, it means sharing the burden with someone else to ensure the parent and child receive the best possible care.

Where Do I Look for Assistance?

Fortunately, there are numerous avenues to explore when seeking assistance. The first crucial step is acknowledging the need for help, followed by creating a plan to obtain the necessary support. Assistance can be found

---

[1] Gates, R., n.d. What are Income Based Clinics - HealthCore Clinic. [online] HealthCore Clinic. Available at: [Accessed 7 September 2022].

through various channels, depending on the specific needs of the parent and child.

Community Clinics

One valuable resource to tap into is the local community. Within the community, there is a wealth of information and access to a range of services, many of which are available at little or no cost. Community clinics are a prime example of such facilities. While some might envision community clinics as inadequately stocked and crowded places for emergency care, this perception is often overly simplified. In reality, community clinics can provide significant benefits to individuals with disabilities and their caregivers.[2]

Many community clinics offer specialized services tailored to disabled adults and their parents. These clinics go beyond the traditional confines of the facility, reaching out to underserved populations in the community. Affordable healthcare options for disabled individuals are also available at community clinics, ensuring access to quality care within their financial means.

Community clinics typically offer a range of medical services, including primary and preventive healthcare, mental and behavioral health support, and social services. They may also provide specialized programs such as physical therapy, occupational therapy, and recreation tailored to individuals with disabilities. By employing staff with specialized training in disability care, community clinics can offer personalized attention and vital assistance to patients while supporting families in their caregiving journey.

Moreover, community clinics often implement a sliding scale charge structure, meaning the amount you are responsible for paying is based on your annual income. This approach ensures that those in need of affordable medical care can access the services they require. (2)

In addition to community resources, there are other avenues to explore for assistance, such as nonprofit organizations, support groups, government agencies, and disability-specific advocacy groups. These organizations often provide valuable information, resources, and support networks for parents and children with disabilities.

It is essential to research and reach out to these various channels early on, even if there is no immediate need for assistance. By familiarizing yourself

---

[2] The Resource Hub at the end of each chapter will list resources discussed.

with available resources and building connections, you can proactively plan for future needs and ensure you are prepared if a crisis arises.

Remember, seeking assistance does not signify a loss of control or responsibility. Instead, it demonstrates the strength and determination to provide the best care possible for your child. By utilizing the support available in the community and beyond, you can lighten the caregiving load and enhance the well-being of both you and your child.

In addition, community health clinics often establish strong connections with local groups that serve individuals with disabilities. This collaboration allows clinic staff to offer valuable information about community resources, support groups, and government programs. They can guide parents through the complex landscape of services available for their disabled children, ensuring they can navigate the system effectively.

Community clinics maintain close relationships with local hospitals and other healthcare providers. This enables them to not only provide medical care but also connect their patients with a wide range of resources and support in various areas. Through partnerships with other organizations, community clinics extend their support services beyond healthcare. They may offer assistance with transportation, financial aid, housing, and collaborate with local initiatives to provide additional resources such as after-school tutoring or job training.

These collaborations make community clinics an invaluable resource for parents and their disabled children. Reaching out to your local community clinic can uncover a wealth of services and support that you may not have been aware of. You might be pleasantly surprised by the level of assistance they can offer, helping you access the necessary care for your child.

Support Groups

Another valuable community resource is support groups. These groups provide a space for individuals with disabilities to come together and share their experiences. Similarly, there are support groups specifically tailored for caregivers of disabled individuals. These groups provide a supportive environment where parents, family members, and other caregivers can connect with others facing similar challenges in caring for disabled loved ones.

Finding the right support group may require some time and exploration, but the effort is well worth it. Building connections with trustworthy individuals who understand your experiences can provide a sense of safety and support.

These relationships offer a platform for sharing advice, seeking guidance, and finding solace in a community that empathizes with the unique journey of caring for a disabled child.

By tapping into community resources such as community clinics and support groups, you can access a network of individuals and organizations dedicated to supporting families like yours. Together, these resources can provide a holistic approach to caregiving, offering not only medical assistance but also emotional support, practical resources, and a sense of belonging.

If you are interested in joining a support group, it is worth discussing the possibility with a medical professional or a health advocate. They may be able to connect you with suitable support groups in your area.

While most support groups are primarily designed for individuals with disabilities, as a caregiver or parent of a person with a disability, you are usually welcome to join many of these groups that offer free access to anyone willing to participate. The purpose is to create a supportive community where individuals can share their experiences and find understanding.

Participating in a support group does not necessarily mean attending every meeting. Some people may find it beneficial to attend meetings only when they are facing challenges, while others may prefer more frequent attendance to enjoy the company of fellow members. Flexibility is key.

Furthermore, physical presence is not always required. Online support groups allow individuals who live in remote areas or have travel limitations to connect with others and engage in chat sessions. Virtual group meetings offer face-to-face conversations using video conferencing platforms. All you need is an internet connection and a webcam to participate from the comfort of your own home.

If your adult child has the intellectual capacity to engage in such relationships, it might be worthwhile to discuss with them the possibility of joining a support group. This can introduce them to new relationships, connections, opportunities, and valuable information that they may appreciate.

Being a part of a support group brings numerous advantages. It can help alleviate some of the pressures that come with being a caregiver, reducing the risk of burnout. Additionally, your child may benefit from knowing that others fully understand and empathize with their mental or physical struggles.

Parent support groups, in particular, provide a space where parents can not only connect with others who can relate to their situation but also share valuable information, provide support, and offer helpful advice and recommendations. Hearing from others who have gone through or are currently experiencing similar challenges can provide a sense of comfort and reassurance.

By joining a support group, you can find solace in the company of others who truly understand, gain insights from their experiences, and receive support and guidance as you navigate the journey of caregiving. It is an opportunity to form meaningful connections, foster personal growth, and find a community that walks alongside you in your caregiving role.

For example, consider the recounted experience of Kelly[3], a parent on the Parent-to-Parent Support Group who said:

"I felt absolutely lost before being able to talk with other parents dealing with the same issues. You think you are completely alone… It is not only debilitating for the child, but the parent as well. When your child has 250+ seizures a day, you are practically hostage at home…I know others are doing it or they have done it too, and then I know I can make it and thrive not just survive this!! There is something comforting about talking with parents who have been through it and understand!"

Or Janice[4], who said:

"When my friend had a problem with a guide dog, she called me to see if I had any ideas, and I told her that I belonged to this really neat group and we ask just about anything and people come up with some great answers.

My friend liked the idea since we are from a small area and not a lot of people know where to turn to. I told her that this group has helped me out on all kinds of different things, and there are times where we just send emails talking about how rough things can get raising a special needs child and we get a "cyber hug."

I am thankful for being part of this great group, without it when there are questions that someone around here can't answer, I know that someone on Parent 2 Parent can at

---

[3] Participant of Parent-to-Parent Support Group.
[4] Participant of Parent-to-Parent Support Group.

least lead me in the right direction or even come up with an answer. Whoever it was that came up with this group needs a "cyber hug" and a huge THANK YOU. Sincerely"

It is essential to learn from others who have faced similar challenges and have taken steps to address them effectively. By engaging with other elderly parents or caregivers, you can inquire about the actions they have taken or are currently implementing to ensure the well-being of their child once they are no longer able to provide care.

Their insights and experiences can offer valuable guidance, and you may discover strategies that you can incorporate into your own plans.

Support group members can also provide valuable information about overcoming difficulties or managing ongoing challenges. By sharing their own experiences, they can offer practical advice and coping strategies that have worked for them. They may have encountered similar obstacles and found effective ways to navigate through them. Engaging with support group members allows you to tap into their knowledge and learn from their experiences.

Furthermore, support group members are a valuable resource for information about other individuals, organizations, or social programs that can provide assistance in obtaining solutions to the challenges you are facing. They can recommend relevant resources, services, or programs that may be beneficial to you and your child.

Building relationships within the support group can also be advantageous. By fostering connections and establishing trust, you may find a support network of individuals who are willing to help if any issues or difficulties arise in the future. These relationships can provide additional support and a sense of security as you navigate the caregiving journey.

Disability Service Centers

Disability service centers play a crucial role in assisting individuals with disabilities and their caregivers. These centers can be established by state governments or private entities with the aim of improving the lives of disabled individuals.

These centers offer a diverse range of services depending on their objectives and available resources. Some serve as informative hubs, connecting individuals with medical opportunities, professional help, and government benefits. Others utilize private or public funding to provide genuine care, such as acquiring assistive devices or offering housing options within supportive communities.

At disability service centers, employees may provide direct services like personal care assistance, respite care, or in-home services. They often employ rehabilitation counselors who specialize in vocational counseling for individuals with disabilities. These counselors assess skills, interests, and abilities to help find suitable employment opportunities. They also facilitate connections with disability support programs and employers willing to hire people with disabilities. Job placement assistance and ongoing support are also provided to ensure successful integration into the workforce.

Furthermore, disability service centers tailor services to specific impairments, catering to individuals with visual, auditory, or cognitive disabilities. These centers also offer valuable guidance and assistance to parents and caregivers in making long-term care plans for their loved ones. They help navigate housing schemes, financial assistance programs, and provide training on independent living skills. Recreational activities and support group introductions are common as well.

Counselors at disability service centers possess extensive expertise and can provide information and referrals to other agencies or organizations as needed. They are knowledgeable about various topics related to disabilities and can assist with specific inquiries. State departments of Social and Health Services can also be contacted for guidance on locating disability service centers in your area.

Technology

Technology has become an invaluable resource for accessing assistance and support. Teleconferencing platforms like Zoom and Skype enable easy connections and information sharing among parents and caregivers. Online forums and communities, such as Scopes, You'reable, and Agingcare, provide spaces for interaction, information, and advice.

Numerous websites and databases offer detailed information about disability services and resources. Online support groups provide a platform for parents to connect with others in similar situations, sharing experiences and advice. Websites like USA Gov, The Arc, Goodwill Industries International, and Parents Helping Parents are examples of valuable online resources.[5]

---

[5] Refer to the Resource Hub at the end of this chapter.

Additionally, technology has produced aids to address specific challenges faced by individuals with disabilities. GPS systems integrated into wheelchairs assist with locating individuals who may wander off. Devices exist to amplify sounds for those with hearing impairments or aid in communication by reading text aloud or translating spoken words. Automatic page turners facilitate reading physical books.

These technological tools can greatly assist disabled individuals, particularly when caregivers are unable to provide a certain level of support. They enhance independence and accessibility, improving the overall quality of life.

By tapping into disability service centers, leveraging technology, and accessing online resources, parents and caregivers can find the assistance, information, and support they need to ensure the well-being of their loved ones with disabilities.

Professionals

Professionals play a crucial role in supporting caregiving parents and their adult children with disabilities. When reaching a point of needing external assistance, various professionals can be relied upon for help and support.

One option is to hire a live-in carer, who is a trained professional providing 24/7 care within the familiar environment of your own home. This arrangement allows your adult child to maintain a level of independence while receiving the necessary care and support on a daily basis. It offers the advantage of avoiding the disruptions associated with institutional care, such as separation from familiar surroundings, the need to give up pets, or adhering to strict schedules.

Having a live-in carer also allows your child to develop a personal bond with a dedicated professional caregiver. This personal relationship can greatly enhance the quality of care provided.

However, it's understandable that some families may have concerns or hesitations about hiring a live-in carer. Factors such as the required minimum commitment of hours per week, limited flexibility in availability, and the associated cost may pose challenges for some families. Privacy concerns and compatibility between the carer and the patient can also be potential issues.

Additionally, news stories about caregivers committing fraud or harming those under their care can be unsettling.[6]

To guarantee the selection of a trustworthy live-in carer, it is essential to follow a comprehensive background check. When assessing the background of a potential carer, you can take the following steps to ensure their suitability for the role:

1. Request a copy of the applicant's ID: Asking for identification helps verify their identity and ensures transparency. It allows you to confirm that they are who they claim to be and helps prevent potential fraud or misrepresentation.

2. Check their criminal history: Utilize online resources such as the National Sex Offender Registry to examine if the applicant has any previous red flags or criminal records. This step is crucial in ensuring the safety and well-being of your loved one.

3. Ask for references: Request references from the applicant and reach out to their previous employers. Speaking with those who have worked with the candidate can provide valuable insights into their work ethic, professionalism, and ability to provide appropriate care.

4. Conduct employment/education history verification: To ensure that the applicant is honest about their qualifications, it is essential to verify their employment and education history. This step helps confirm their past experiences and educational background.

5. Conduct a drug screening: Considering the safety of your loved one, conducting a drug screening can help identify if the applicant is using substances that may jeopardize their ability to provide proper care. It is recommended to perform pre-employment drug testing once a conditional job offer has been made, following guidelines provided by the Equal Employment Opportunity Commission (EEOC).

6. Conduct a driving history verification: If driving is part of the caregiver's responsibilities, it is important to review their driving record. Checking for a clean driving history helps ensure the safety of your loved one during transportation.

---

[6] UK Care Guide. 2022. ADVANTAGES & DISADVANTAGES OF LIVE IN CARE 2022 - What are they? [online] [Accessed 7 September 2022]

By following these steps, you can gain a comprehensive understanding of the prospective carer's background, qualifications, and suitability for the caregiving role.

This process helps mitigate risks, ensures the well-being of your loved one, and provides peace of mind for you as a caregiver. Taking these precautions can help alleviate concerns and provide peace of mind when hiring a live-in carer for your adult child.

If a live-in carer is not the right option for your situation, there are alternative categories of professionals who can provide valuable assistance. One such option is hiring a home health aide, who is a specially trained professional offering in-home care for individuals with chronic illnesses, disabilities, or cognitive impairments.

Home health aides can be a tremendous support for parents of children with disabilities, as they help with essential daily activities like bathing, dressing, grooming, and using the restroom. Additionally, they may assist with meal preparation, light housekeeping, medication management, and transportation to medical appointments. Many families prefer hiring a home health aide due to the increased privacy and flexibility it offers.

When considering a home health aide for your child, it is important to conduct interviews with multiple candidates and thoroughly check their references. Clear communication of expectations and specific instructions regarding your child's care is crucial as well.

Another option to consider is finding a respite carer who can temporarily take over the caregiving responsibilities, allowing you to take a much-needed break. Respite care providers can offer overnight stays, daytime visits, or longer-term stays depending on your specific needs. This arrangement not only gives families respite from the demands of caregiving but also ensures that disabled children receive one-on-one attention and care when their primary caregiver is unavailable.

On-call emergency services are also a valuable resource for assistance in caring for your child. These services provide peace of mind, knowing that help is readily available in case of an emergency. Additionally, equipping your child with a personal emergency response system (PERS) can be beneficial. PERS devices are wearable and have an emergency button that, when activated, contacts the on-call emergency service, which promptly dispatches assistance.

It is also important to recognize that there is a wide range of specialists available who can provide tailored assistance to support your child to live with their disability. Whether it is consulting with a psychiatrist or psychologist for intellectual development disabilities or seeking the expertise of a physiotherapist for physical development or movement issues, medical professionals are ready to assist when specialized care and treatment are required.

Moreover, professionals from various fields can help families navigate complex areas such as housing, community living, insurance coverage, and medical bills. They can provide guidance on the best ways to care for a disabled child and inform you about available assistance options. Furthermore, these specialists can connect families with support groups and other valuable resources to make the caregiving and receiving experience more manageable.

In addition to live-in carers, there are other professionals who can assist in various aspects of caregiving. These professionals may include:

- **Medical specialists**: Doctors, therapists, and nurses who can provide medical assessments, treatments, and therapies tailored to your adult child's specific needs.

- **Social workers**: These professionals can offer guidance on accessing community resources, financial assistance programs, and support services. They can also provide emotional support and help navigate complex systems.

- **Legal advisors**: Lawyers specializing in disability law can assist in establishing guardianship, creating trusts, and ensuring your child's legal rights are protected.

- **Financial advisors:** Professionals who specialize in financial planning for individuals with disabilities can help manage financial resources, navigate government benefits, and plan for future care needs.

It's essential to engage with these professionals based on your specific requirements and seek their expertise to ensure the well-being and future planning for your adult child with a disability.

Service Animals

If you have reached a point where your disabled loved one requires more supervision than you can provide, considering a service animal might be a viable option. Service animals, as defined by the Americans with Disabilities Act (ADA), are dogs that have undergone individual training to perform specific tasks or chores that benefit individuals with disabilities. These disabilities can encompass physical, sensory, psychiatric, intellectual, or other mental conditions. The tasks performed by service animals vary widely, ranging from assisting individuals in wheelchairs to retrieving objects, alerting them to sounds, and even reminding someone to take medication.

Service animals are trained for various purposes, such as guiding the blind, alerting their owners to approaching individuals from behind, and providing stability for those with walking difficulties. Additionally, there are service animals specifically trained to assist individuals who experience seizures.

If you are considering getting a service animal, there are several organizations you can reach out to. Assistance Dogs International, the International Dog Guide Federation, and the Paws4People Foundation are just a few examples of organizations that provide service animals. These organizations can provide information, guidance, and assistance in obtaining a service animal that suits the specific needs of your disabled area.[7]

It is important to note that acquiring a service animal involves a comprehensive process that includes assessment, training, and matching the animal to the individual's needs. The organizations mentioned above have expertise in this area and can guide you through the necessary steps to ensure a successful partnership between the individual and their service animal.

Service animals can offer significant support and enhance the quality of life for individuals with disabilities. However, it is essential to thoroughly research and consider the specific requirements and responsibilities associated with having a service animal. Proper training, care, and ongoing support are crucial for maintaining the well-being and effectiveness of the service animal in assisting your disabled loved one.

It is crucial to remember that you and your family are not alone in facing the challenges that come with caring for a disabled child. There are numerous resources and support systems available to help you navigate this journey successfully. The key is to identify the right assistance that aligns with your child's specific needs and your family's circumstances.

Don't hesitate to seek help and reach out to individuals, organizations, and professionals who specialize in providing support to families like yours.

---

[7] Refer to Resource Hub at the end of this chapter.

They have the knowledge, experience, and willingness to assist you in any way possible. Whether it's finding the right caregiver, accessing home health aides, considering a service animal, or connecting with specialists, there are solutions out there waiting for you.

Remember that asking for help is not a sign of weakness but a testament to your dedication and commitment to providing the best care for your child. By seeking support, you can alleviate some of the burdens and challenges you face, while also ensuring that your child receives the care and assistance they deserve.

No matter how overwhelming the journey may seem at times, know that there is hope and support available. Embrace the opportunity to reach out, ask questions, and connect with those who can offer guidance and understanding. Together, you can find the right solutions and create a better future for your child and your family.

Resource Hub:

Low-Cost Clinics Locators

The UK is not included in this section because the NHS covers all public healthcare costs for English residents.

Organization	Website/Contact Line/Mail	Location	Special Note
Needy Meds	https://www.needymeds.org/medical-clinics 800-503-6897 info@needymeds.org	USA	This isn't an actual clinic. It's simply a resource for finding local clinics near you.
Free Clinic	https://www.freeclinics.com/ (541)715-3900 support@freeclinics.com	USA	Online resource
The Healthline	https://www.thehealthline.ca/	Canada	Online resource
Reach Community Health Center	https://www.reachcentre.bc.ca/ basic4health@reachcentre.bc.ca	Canada	Physical organization
Muslim Welfare Center	https://www.muslimwelfarecentre.com/causes/free-clinic/ freeclinic@mwcanada.com (647) 641-1027	Canada	This center is primarily based in Ontario, residents in other provinces can reach out to them to access possible networks in their locale.

Support Groups

Organization	Website/Line/Email	Location	Special Note
Mommies of Miracle	http://mommiesofmiracles.com/ https://www.facebook.com/MommiesofMiracles	Virtual	The support group caters to the needs of mothers who have children of all ages.
Special Parents Information Network (SPIN)	https://www.spinsc.org/support-groups (831) 722-2800	Virtual	This is a network of caregivers that connects you with other carers through a determined schedule. The service is bilingual i.e English and Spanish
Parent 2 Parent	https://www.p2pusa.org/parents/	USA	This organization pairs you up with another parent close to you and helps you form accessible, quality, and personalized connections.
Parents of Adults with Developmental Disabilities and Other Support Needs	https://www.facebook.com/groups/pacdd	Online	This is a group dedicated for parents of adults with disabilities.
Center For Parents Information and Resources	https://www.parentcenterhub.org/parentgroups/ (973) 642-8100	Online	This database provides information on several helpful points such as where to find a support group, disability-related resources, and updates on live programs in various places that you can attend.
Aspergers/Autism Network	https://www.aane.org/resources/family-and-friends/ https://www.aane.org/online-forums/	Online	This resource helps you access a wide range of support groups for all kind of caregiver roles for persons with intellectual disabilities.
Embracing Life	https://embracing.life/article/facebook-groups-for-christian-special-needs-parents	Online	This resource is not an actual support group, but it contains a very helpful list for anyone looking to build a Christian based support network.
Singing Through The Rain	https://singingthroughtherain.net/2015/10/groups-for-special-needs-families.html	Online	This resource provides helpful links to groups for parents of children with special needs. The list contains everything from support groups for discussions to groups for sharing useful items.
Bayada	https://blog.bayada.com/be-healthy/eight-support-groups-for-parents-raising-children-with-special-needs	Online	This is not an actual support group, but it contains a very helpful list for anyone looking to build an easily accessible support network.

Mental Care and Home Care Resources

Yourable	https://livingmadeeasy.org.uk/about-us/youreable	online	An online community support and resources.
AgingCare	https://www.agingcare.com/	online	Free assessment. In home care & resources.
Chatowl	https://chatowl.com/	online	Virtual Mental Health Therapist
Elomia	https://elomia.com/	online	Virtual Mental Health Therapist
Youper	https://www.youper.ai/	online	Ai Mental Health Therapist
7 Cups	https://www.7cups.com/	Free online	Free Emotional Support
Bliss (CIMHS)	https://cimhs.com/bliss-free-online-therapy-for-depression.html	Free online	Free Therapy for Depression
Ginger	https://www.ginger.com/	online	Mental health coaching
Other Resources	**For Home and Life**	online	
OWL	https://owlinc.net/about/	Physical location-Kentucky	Workshop for individuals with severe disabilities.
The ARC	https://thearc.org/	Physical & Online	Advocacy and resources.
Parents Helping Parents	https://www.php.com/	Physical & Online	Support for families with disabilities.
International Dog Guide Federation	https://www.igdf.org.uk/	Physical & Online	Information and resources.
Paws4People Foundation	https://paws4people.org/	Physical & Online	Information and resources.

FOUR

SECURING FINANCES

How Can I Ensure the Security of My Finances?

For the majority of individuals, financial security encompasses various aspects that contribute to a stable and comfortable life. Being debt-free, having sufficient funds to pursue personal goals, providing education for children, owning a desirable home, and overall well-being are key elements of financial security. However, for some, such as parents of disabled children, financial security extends even further, encompassing the assurance of their own and their children's well-being beyond their own lifetime.

Considering this reality, it is crucial to initiate financial planning as early as possible if you haven't done so already, in order to secure your finances and provide for your child's future. Additionally, if you feel that you are not saving enough money, it is important to explore ways to increase your income and reduce expenses. By starting early, you can benefit from the advantages of time in growing your wealth.

There are two fundamental approaches to increasing your finances: increasing your income and reducing your expenditure. This chapter explores how you can effectively implement these strategies to build a solid financial foundation.

Investments

Investing is a remarkable avenue to enhance your financial security. However, it is vital to exercise caution, as certain investments carry high returns but also substantial risks. Engaging in investments that pose significant risk can be unwise and potentially devastating to your financial situation.

When seeking secure investment options, it is prudent to consider those that align with your age and the presence of dependents, such as an insurance policy. For instance, a survivorship annuity can provide a guaranteed source of income later in life, ensuring that even if you pass away before receiving all the installments, your child will still be entitled to receive the payments. If feasible, opting for a lump sum annuity can be beneficial, as it fulfills the annuity's requirements in a single payment, safeguarding your child's financial well-being in the event of unforeseen circumstances.

Another valuable option is a life insurance policy that sufficiently covers your child's financial needs in the event of your demise. This guarantees that your child will be taken care of financially, providing you with peace of mind.

Treasury bills and bonds are secure investment choices worth considering. These government-issued IOUs are regarded as highly reliable, as the government does not default on them. Treasury bills are short-term investments that mature within a year or less, while bonds have longer maturity periods, often up to 30 years. Although bonds may have a longer-term payout, they can be inherited by your child, offering long-term financial stability. These investment options carry relatively low risks and can yield high returns.

Asset protection trusts offer an additional method to safeguard your assets. These trusts are specifically designed to shield assets from creditors, providing protection even in the event of bankruptcy. By holding assets in a trust rather than in your own name, you can ensure their preservation.

It is crucial to note that using such methods must be done ethically and without fraudulent intent, as there may be severe consequences for fraudulent actions.

Regardless of the approach you choose, it is essential to consult with licensed financial and legal professionals to ensure that you are making the most advantageous decisions for both yourself and your child's future. Their expertise will provide you with confidence in pursuing the most suitable options to secure your finances effectively.

Fundraisers

Fundraisers offer another avenue to enhance your financial security. As mentioned in the previous chapter, seeking assistance should never be seen as a weakness, and engaging in fundraisers is a way to receive financial support when needed. Let's take a look at an inspiring example involving Tara, her family, and their support network. They organized a comprehensive fundraising plan that incorporated various creative ideas. They hired a hypnotist for an entertaining show where people could donate money to the cause, arranged a 40-kilometer charity walk, and even organized a "crazy hair day" event. Through their collective efforts, they successfully raised the required funds within a few months.

This example highlights several valuable lessons. Firstly, it emphasizes the importance of not hesitating to seek help when facing financial challenges. Secondly, it underscores the significance of support from close friends and family. Lastly, it demonstrates that a successful fundraising campaign often requires multiple action plans to achieve its goals. Thus, it is crucial to explore various avenues when endeavoring to raise funds.

Online fundraising campaigns are another avenue worth considering. Platforms like GoFundMe, Kickstarter, and FundRazr have proven instrumental in helping individuals in need gather financial support for their causes.[8] When launching an online fundraiser, it is essential to craft a compelling story and accompany it with engaging photos or videos. Additionally, effective marketing of your campaign is crucial to ensure its visibility to potential donors. If executed correctly, an online fundraiser can supplement your income and cover certain expenses for both you and your child.

If you are uncomfortable being the face of the fundraising campaign, rest assured that there are alternative approaches that do not require you to be in the spotlight. For instance, you can collaborate with other seniors or parents of disabled children to reach out to charitable organizations. These organizations can organize events where donated goods or services are silently auctioned off. Additionally, local volunteers can contribute by participating in fundraising bake sales or car washes.

Larger nonprofit organizations can also be valuable allies in your fundraising efforts. They often host events such as walks or runs, where participants collect pledges from sponsors. Moreover, galas and social gatherings provide enjoyable opportunities to raise funds while fostering a sense of community.

Participating in these activities enables you to generate financial resources

---

[8] Refer to the Resource Hub at the end of this chapter.

for your future without necessarily drawing attention to yourself. Furthermore, you may find joy in engaging in fun and fulfilling experiences while contributing to your financial security.

Downsizing

As individuals age, they often find that their homes have become too large for their needs, particularly when their non-disabled children have moved out and established their own households. The expenses associated with maintaining and repairing a large house, as well as the high costs of heating and cooling, can be burdensome for older individuals. In such cases, downsizing to a smaller and more affordable home or apartment can be a wise financial decision that should not be overlooked.

This is especially true if you currently reside in a large house that demands significant financial resources for its upkeep. If you are living alone with only your child, there may be no need to maintain such a spacious property. By downsizing, you can reduce various expenses, including mortgage payments, property taxes, maintenance costs, and utilities.

Downsizing not only leads to lower living expenses but also presents an opportunity to release equity from your home, which can contribute to your retirement savings and future care provisions for your disabled child. Additionally, downsizing provides an opportunity to declutter and let go of belongings that are no longer used or essential. This may include clothing, furniture, or sentimental items that hold memories of a deceased spouse. While parting with such possessions can be emotionally challenging, it is important to remember that you are making these changes for the betterment of both yourself and your child's well-being.

Furthermore, selling or donating these items can generate additional income or assist others in need. By reducing the clutter in your life, you create a more organized and financially efficient living environment.

Although downsizing may require effort and adjustment, the long-term benefits make it worthwhile. In fact, you may even discover that downsizing liberates you and allows for a simpler and happier life.

If the thought of downsizing still makes you uncomfortable, consider the possibility of renting out a room in your house to boarders. This arrangement not only provides companionship for you and your child but also brings in extra income each month. Services like Roomster and Airbnb can help you connect with potential boarders.

However, it is crucial to exercise caution and conduct thorough background checks on potential tenants. Requesting references and speaking to their friends, family, and previous landlords can provide valuable insights into their character and reliability as tenants. Additionally, performing a credit check can help assess their financial responsibility and likelihood of paying rent on time.

Establish clear expectations regarding rent payments, house rules, and the length of the boarder's stay. By doing so, you can maintain your autonomy, privacy, and financial stability while welcoming a new person into your home.

Renting out a room not only offers financial benefits but also creates an opportunity for positive social interaction and support within your household.

Downsizing one's home can be a significant life decision that offers numerous benefits, including financial savings, reduced maintenance, and a simplified lifestyle. If you're considering downsizing, here are some suggestions on how to proceed and organizations you can contact to assist you in the process:

1. Assess your needs: Begin by evaluating your current housing situation and determining your needs. Consider factors such as the size of your home, maintenance requirements, accessibility, proximity to amenities, and your future goals. This assessment will help you establish criteria for your downsized home.

2. Create a plan: Develop a clear plan outlining your downsizing goals, timeline, and budget. Determine the ideal location, size, and features you desire in your new home. Consider consulting with a financial advisor or real estate professional to help you assess the financial implications and explore options within your budget.

3. Declutter and organize: Downsizing provides an excellent opportunity to declutter your belongings and simplify your life. Sort through your possessions and decide what to keep, donate, sell, or discard. Be mindful of sentimental items but try to prioritize functionality and practicality. This process can be emotionally challenging, so seek support from friends or family if needed.

4. Seek professional assistance: Several organizations can provide guidance and support throughout the downsizing process. Contact a senior move manager or downsizing specialist who can help you plan, declutter, pack, and coordinate your move. These professionals have expertise in managing the logistics and emotional aspects of downsizing.

5. Explore housing options: Research various housing options that align with your downsizing goals. Consider ADA accessible and compliant apartments, condominiums, townhouses, or smaller single-family homes. Visit different properties to assess their suitability and amenities. Engage with real estate agents specializing in downsizing to assist you in finding the right home.

6. Contact local charities and thrift stores: When decluttering, consider donating unwanted items to local charities or thrift stores. They can benefit from your donations, and it helps reduce waste. Reach out to organizations such as Goodwill, Salvation Army, or Habitat for Humanity to arrange for pick-up or drop-off of your donations.

7. Utilize online platforms for selling: If you have valuable items that you no longer need, consider selling them online through platforms like eBay, Craigslist, or Facebook Marketplace. This can help you generate extra income while decluttering your home.

8. Seek support from family and friends: Downsizing can be an overwhelming process, both physically and emotionally. Reach out to family and friends for assistance and emotional support. They can help you pack, move, or provide advice during this transition.

9. Take it one step at a time: Downsizing is a gradual process. Break it down into smaller tasks and tackle them one at a time. Celebrate each milestone and acknowledge the progress you're making.

Consider downsizing as an opportunity for a fresh start and a more manageable living situation. Approach the process with a positive mindset and be open to the possibilities that a smaller home can offer.

Food Stamps

In recent times, various factors such as the Covid-19 pandemic's aftermath, increased transportation costs, and conflicts impacting food-producing nations have led to a significant surge in food prices. This has created a temptation for individuals to compromise on meals in order to manage their food expenses. While saving money is commendable, it should never come at the expense of essential nutrition. Thankfully, many countries and states provide aid through food stamps and other programs aimed at combating hunger. Unfortunately, there are negative attitudes surrounding the use of food stamps that prevent people from benefiting from the valuable support they provide. Some view food stamps as handouts or associate them with laziness and a reluctance to work. However, these misconceptions are far from the truth.

The reality is that the cost of maintaining a nutritious diet has significantly increased, while income levels have not risen proportionally to meet these expenses. In such circumstances, it is both economically and sensibly prudent to take advantage of available assistance through food stamps and similar programs, both in the short and long term.

If you find yourself with a low income, it is essential to let go of any negative beliefs about food assistance programs and utilize them to ensure that you and your child do not face nutritional deprivation. By saving money through food stamps, you can allocate those funds towards other necessary expenses. Moreover, it prevents the need to spend money on medical bills and treatments that may arise from complications resulting from inadequate nutrition.

Additionally, access to food stamps relieves the pressure and anxiety associated with wondering where the next meal will come from. In countries like the USA, food stamp programs often offer extended support periods for individuals with disabilities and their households. This ensures that they have consistent access to quality nutrition during financially challenging times.

It is crucial to recognize that food stamps and similar programs are designed to support individuals and families in need, promoting their well-being and ensuring their basic needs are met. Accepting this assistance not only addresses immediate food security concerns but also allows individuals to focus on other aspects of their lives without constantly worrying about their next meal.

By embracing the available help and shifting away from negative perceptions, you can provide yourself and your child with the nourishment necessary for a healthy and fulfilling life.

SNAP

Government food stamps, officially known as the Supplemental Nutrition Assistance Program (SNAP), provide crucial assistance to individuals and families who struggle to afford nutritious food. SNAP aims to alleviate food insecurity and promote better nutrition among low-income households in the United States. If you find yourself in a situation where you need support to meet your basic food needs, applying for SNAP can be a valuable option.

To apply for SNAP benefits, you can start by visiting your state's SNAP website or the official SNAP page on the U.S. Department of Agriculture's website. The process typically involves filling out an application form that asks for information about your household, income, expenses, and other relevant details. Alternatively, you can apply in person at your local SNAP office or by phone, depending on your state's procedures.

Eligibility for SNAP benefits are determined based on several factors, including income, household size, expenses, and assets. Generally, households with limited income and resources are more likely to qualify. Income limits vary depending on the state and household size, but typically, your gross monthly income should be at or below 130% of the federal poverty level. Some states also consider net income and have different guidelines for households with elderly or disabled members.

It's important to note that eligibility requirements and benefit amounts can differ from state to state, so it's recommended to check the specific guidelines for your state. Additionally, certain groups, such as elderly individuals, people with disabilities, and those receiving certain other public assistance programs, may have different criteria or exemptions that make them eligible for SNAP.

When applying for SNAP, be prepared to provide necessary documentation such as identification, proof of income, utility bills, rent or mortgage statements, and any other relevant information that may support your application. The application process typically involves an interview with a caseworker who will review your eligibility and help determine your benefit amount.

If you're unsure about the application process or need assistance, many local community organizations, food banks, and social service agencies offer support to individuals applying for SNAP benefits. They can provide guidance, help with the application, and answer any questions you may have.

Recall that, SNAP is designed to provide temporary assistance during challenging times, so if your circumstances change, it's important to update your information promptly. Regularly assessing your eligibility and staying informed about any policy updates or changes can ensure that you continue to receive the necessary support for you and your family's nutritional needs.

Community Food Pantries

Community food pantries are essential resources that provide food assistance to individuals and families facing food insecurity. They are typically nonprofit organizations, often run by volunteers, that collect and distribute food to those in need within a specific community or region. These food pantries play a vital role in ensuring that individuals and families have access to nutritious meals when they face financial difficulties or cannot afford an adequate food supply.

The primary beneficiaries of community food pantries are individuals and families experiencing food insecurity. This can include low-income households, unemployed individuals, seniors on fixed incomes, single-parent families, and individuals facing unexpected financial crises. Food pantries serve as a temporary support system to help bridge the gap between limited resources and the need for nourishing meals.

Community food pantries are facilitated by dedicated individuals, volunteers, and staff members who contribute their time and efforts to ensure the smooth operation of the pantry. These individuals often work in collaboration with local organizations, such as churches, community centers, or social service agencies, to secure donations, manage inventory, and distribute food to those in need. Some food pantries also receive support from government programs, grants, or partnerships with larger food banks.

Locating community food pantries in your area is relatively straightforward. Here are a few methods to help you find local food pantries:

1. Online search: Use search engines to find food pantries near you. Look for keywords such as "community food pantry" or "food assistance" followed by the name of your city or region.

2. Food bank directories: Many regions have food bank networks or directories that provide information on local food pantries. Visit the website of your local food bank or food assistance organization to access their directory or contact information.

3. Social service agencies: Reach out to local social service agencies, such as welfare offices, homeless shelters, or community centers. They often have knowledge of and can provide information about nearby food pantries.

4. Hotline services: Some areas have dedicated helpline services or hotlines that connect individuals with food assistance resources. These helplines can provide information on the locations and operating hours of nearby food pantries.

5. Community outreach programs: Stay informed about community events, fairs, or gatherings where organizations might distribute information about local food pantries. Local newspapers, bulletin boards, or community newsletters are also good sources for such information.

Once you have located a nearby food pantry, reach out to them directly to inquire about their services, eligibility criteria, and any required documentation. Many food pantries have specific operating hours or appointment systems, so it's essential to familiarize yourself with their procedures to access their assistance effectively.

Keep in mind that community food pantries are there to provide support and ensure that nobody goes hungry. Do not hesitate to reach out to them when you or your family are facing food insecurity or limited access to nutritious meals.

Disability Grants

An effective way to significantly improve your financial situation is to consider the options available in the form of disability grants. These grants can be provided by either the government, private organizations, or even generous individuals.

Grants can sometimes be quite substantial in amount, and they have the potential to provide an extra financial boost while assisting you in planning for your child's future. However, it is important to note that there are no guarantees when it comes to grants, and you may need to apply for multiple grants before receiving positive results. Nevertheless, it is worth exploring and applying for them.

One valuable tip is to be specific and targeted in your grant applications. For instance, if your child has a visual impairment, it would be more advantageous to apply for grants such as LVRN, Victa, or SightFirst, which are specifically designed to address challenges related to visual impairments. Similarly, if your child has a physical disability, grants from organizations like Im Able or the Kelly Brush Foundation would be more appropriate.[9]

---

[9] Refer to the Resource Hub at the end of this chapter.

Additionally, leveraging specificity can also be beneficial when applying for grants that cater to specific needs. Some grants are tailored to address requirements such as housing, education, or the acquisition of assistive devices. Hence, it is advisable to explore and apply for grants that align with your child's specific needs.

Even if you currently feel that your child does not require these grants because you can easily cover such expenses, it might be wise to register them for such grants in the future. This proactive step can ensure that they have access to financial support, enabling them to lead fulfilling lives both presently and in the years to come.

Another option to consider is multi-purpose grants, which may not be as substantial as specialized grants but can still provide a financial boost to your circumstances.

Some examples of general grants that you could explore for your child include Supplemental Security Income (SSI), Social Security Disability Insurance (SSDI), and others. Who knows, luck might just be on your side and grant you a positive outcome.

Work From Home Opportunities & Exchanges

In the previous chapter, we discussed how you can assist your child in finding remote employment. However, who says you can't explore work-from-home opportunities yourself and earn some extra income?

While your child's work may involve using assistive devices and computers, your own work can be something physical and enjoyable but not physically demanding. For instance, if you have a love for animals, you could transform your home into a doggy day-care service and establish a business taking care of your neighbors' pets. If you have a talent for baking, you could start a small, customized bakery and create pastries for customers. Alternatively, if you possess a knack for fixing things, you could consider setting up a small repair shop.

Time Banks-Exchange

You can also capitalize on your skills and save money by trading your skills or time. Creating a Time Bank with other parents of children with disabilities is an excellent way to do this. Time banks are systems where individuals exchange services, accumulating hours for the services they provide, which they can later use when they require assistance. For instance, you might offer transportation, housecleaning, or cooking services to a neighbor and "bank" the hours. Later on, you can "cash them in" when you need someone to perform a service such as yard work or grocery shopping. Time banks not only provide valuable services to individuals who may be unable to perform certain tasks but also help save money on expensive services like transportation and reduce stress for others by taking care of activities that might be inconvenient for them.

Furthermore, time banks foster a sense of community and belonging among their members. If you are interested in establishing something that caters to the needs of disabled individuals, you could create a recreational center for disabled people, which could also operate as a non-profit organization that receives donations from the community. The proceeds from the center can be invested in facilities that benefit disabled individuals who frequent the center. This initiative could also keep your child occupied, and other parents of disabled children are likely to be interested and willing to contribute to running the center.

If official Time Bank services are not available in your area, you can always engage in the traditional bartering system with people close to you. For example, if you excel at knitting, you could knit a pair of socks for your neighbor in exchange for them walking your dog three times a week. Or if you struggle to find time for grocery shopping, you could ask your neighbor to do it for you in exchange for cooking a meal for them once a week.

If you have professional credentials and expertise in a relevant industry, you may also want to put them to use. You may set up a home-based consulting practice, for instance, or provide basic bookkeeping to local startups.

The possibilities for work-from-home opportunities are endless; you simply need to be creative and find something you enjoy doing that allows you to stay at home and care for your child.

A TimeBanking organization is a community-based initiative that promotes the exchange of services and skills among its members. The fundamental concept behind TimeBanking is the belief that everyone's time and skills have value, and by engaging in reciprocal exchanges, strong support networks can be built within communities.

In a TimeBank, individuals earn one-time credit for each hour they spend helping others. This credit can then be redeemed to receive assistance or services from other members of the TimeBank. The principle is simple: one hour of helping another person earns one-time credit, regardless of the specific service provided.

TimeBanking encourages a shift in focus away from monetary transactions and towards values that hold greater significance, such as family, social justice, and the preservation of democratic processes. By participating in a TimeBank, individuals can contribute to their community while simultaneously receiving support and assistance when needed.

To find TimeBank listings and information, there are several resources available. One option is to search online for local TimeBank organizations in your area. Many TimeBanks have their own websites or social media pages where they provide details about their services, membership requirements, and upcoming events. Local community centers, libraries, or city government offices may also have information about TimeBanking initiatives in the area.

Furthermore, there are online platforms and directories specifically dedicated to TimeBanking. These platforms serve as a hub for various TimeBanks, allowing individuals to join and participate in multiple TimeBanking communities. They often provide comprehensive listings of active TimeBanks, their contact information, and the services they offer.

When considering joining TimeBank, it's important to review their guidelines, membership agreements, and any fees or requirements that may be in place. Each TimeBank operates independently, so the specifics can vary from one organization to another.

By engaging in TimeBanking, individuals can build stronger connections within their communities, foster a sense of mutual support, and rediscover the importance of non-monetary values. It offers a unique approach to social interaction and resource sharing, promoting a more inclusive and equitable society. Timebanks link is listed in the Resource Hub.

Aligning with your abilities-

Work-from-home opportunities can be beneficial for both baby boomers and their adult children with disabilities, providing flexibility, independence, and the ability to earn income from the comfort of their own homes. While the specific opportunities may depend on the individual's abilities and circumstances, here are some potential work-at-home options suitable for both baby boomers and their adult children with a disability.

1. Freelancing: Baby boomers and individuals with disabilities can leverage their skills and expertise by offering freelance services in various fields. This can include writing, graphic design, web development, virtual assistance, consulting, and more. Freelancing allows individuals to work on their own terms and take on projects that align with their abilities and interests.

2. Online Selling: Setting up an online store or utilizing platforms like Etsy or eBay can be a great option for selling handmade crafts, vintage items, or unique products. Baby boomers and individuals with disabilities can showcase their creativity and entrepreneurial spirit while managing their own online business.

3. Virtual Tutoring: If you have knowledge in a particular subject, you can consider offering virtual tutoring services. This can be done through video conferencing platforms, where you can provide one-on-one or group tutoring sessions to students of all ages.

4. Remote Customer Service: Many companies hire remote customer service representatives to handle customer inquiries and provide support. This can be done through phone, email, or live chat. Baby boomers and individuals with disabilities with strong communication skills can excel in such roles.

5. Online Surveys and Market Research: Participating in online surveys and market research studies can be a simple and flexible way to earn extra income. There are several websites and platforms that connect individuals with survey opportunities and compensate them for their time and opinions.

6. Content Creation: Creating and monetizing content through platforms like YouTube, blogs, podcasts, or social media can be a rewarding work-from-home opportunity. Whether it's sharing personal experiences, providing advice, or showcasing talents, individuals can generate income through advertising, sponsorships, or crowdfunding.

7. Remote Healthcare and Counseling Services: Baby boomers with healthcare or counseling backgrounds can explore remote opportunities to provide telehealth services, online therapy, or counseling sessions. This can be especially beneficial for individuals with disabilities who may prefer virtual consultations.

8. Transcription and Data Entry: For individuals with good typing skills and attention to detail, transcription and data entry work can be done remotely. Many companies and organizations hire remote workers for tasks such as transcribing audio recordings or inputting data into spreadsheets or databases.

It's important to note that the suitability of these opportunities may vary depending on the specific abilities, interests, and qualifications of individuals. It's advisable to assess individual strengths and preferences before pursuing any work-from-home option. Additionally, individuals may need to consider any legal or regulatory requirements associated with their chosen field of work.

It's essential for severely disabled individuals to explore opportunities that align with their abilities, interests, and support needs. Accommodations such as adaptive equipment, assistive technology, or flexible work arrangements may be necessary to ensure success in these roles.

Moreover, individuals should consider their legal rights, eligibility for government programs or benefits, and any potential impact on existing benefits when engaging in work-from-home opportunities.

By embracing work-from-home opportunities, baby boomers and their adult child with disabilities can tap into their skills, passions, and expertise while enjoying the flexibility and independence that remote work provides—all while working in an environment that accommodates their specific needs.

To sum it all up-

There are various strategies to enhance your financial situation, both in the short term and the long term. Alongside managing your expenses wisely, it is crucial to explore funding opportunities to support your financial goals.

In the short term, you can consider taking up temporary or part-time jobs, renting out space in your home, or initiating a small-scale business venture. Engaging in bartering arrangements with community members can also be beneficial, as it allows for the exchange of services without involving monetary transactions.

For long-term financial stability, you can explore options such as downsizing your living arrangements, reviewing, and optimizing your insurance coverage, applying for grants or fundraising opportunities, and researching government assistance programs that may provide additional support.

Regardless of your current financial circumstances, it is important to approach the situation with creativity and resourcefulness. Remember to maintain a positive outlook and not lose hope. Financial improvement takes time, so focus on making progress step by step, day by day. By remaining persistent and resilient, you can achieve better financial stability in the future.

Resource Hub

Funding and Grants

There are several grants available for disabled person and they are too numerous to mention here. However, the hub below provides helpful links and pointers on grants you could look into applying for.

Organization	Website	Notes
Navigate Life	https://www.navigatelifetexas.org/en/insurance-financial-help/funding-grants-for-children-with-disabilities	Grants
United Spinal Association	https://askusresourcecenter.unitedspinal.org/index.php?pg=kb.page&id=3036	Grants
Braun Ability	https://www.braunability.com/us/en/blog/funding-and-financing/grants-for-families-with-disabled-children.html	Grant Locator
Grants For Medical	https://www.grantsformedical.com/grants-for-parents-with-a-disabled-child.html	Grants
Kidspeech	https://www.kidspeech.com/programs/special-needs-grants/	Grants
Well Child	https://www.wellchild.org.uk/get-support/information-hub/grants-for-families/	Grants
Sight First	https://www.lionsclubs.org/en/start-our-approach/grant-types/sightfirst-grants	Vision Impaired
VICTA	https://www.victa.org.uk/our-services/grants/	Vision Impaired
LVRN	https://www.lionsvisionresource.org/about-us/	Vision Impaired
IM Able	https://imablefoundation.org/	Physically Impaired
GoFundMe	https://www.gofundme.com/	Fundraiser
TimeBanks	https://timebanks.org/what-is-timebanking/	Work Exchange
Go Fund Me	https://www.gofundme.com/	Fund raiser platform.
Kick Starter	https://www.kickstarter.com/	Fund raiser platform.
Fundrazr	https://fundrazr.com/	Fund raiser platform.

FIVE

MENTAL WELLNESS

How to Manage and Support My Own Mental Health?

As a caregiver, your role is indispensable when it comes to ensuring the good health and overall well-being of your child. However, it's crucial to recognize that taking care of your own mental health is equally essential. Caregivers are particularly susceptible to the development of depression due to the considerable anxiety and stress that often accompanies the responsibility of caring for a loved one with a disability.

The reasons behind this vulnerability are not difficult to understand. Firstly, caregivers frequently prioritize the needs of their loved ones over their own, sometimes neglecting their own well-being in the process. The rare moments they manage to allocate for self-care can be clouded by feelings of guilt and insecurity about their child's welfare.

Secondly, caregivers often find themselves with limited time for socialization. Over time, this isolation from friends and family can lead to a growing sense of loneliness and disconnection from their support networks.

Lastly, caregivers may be exposed to traumatic events, such as witnessing their children in moments of helplessness, pain, and the inability to perform daily tasks independently. These experiences can accumulate over the years, taking a toll on the caregiver's mental health, sometimes without them even realizing it.

This chapter delves into the significance of safeguarding your mental health as a caregiver. It discusses how to identify signs of mental health decline and provides practical guidance on what steps to take when your mental well-being is not at its best. The well-being of both you and your loved one is interconnected, and maintaining your own mental health is not just a matter of personal care but an essential component of being an effective caregiver.

Why Does My Mental Health Hold Significant Importance?

All too often, people place a strong emphasis on their physical well-being while inadvertently neglecting the state of their mental health. As a caregiver, it's not only a responsibility to yourself but also to your child or ward to ensure that your mental and emotional well-being is in good shape when providing care. There are numerous compelling reasons why your mental health should be a priority in your caregiving journey.

First and foremost, maintaining good mental health significantly reduces the risk of experiencing burnout. When you're mentally healthy, you are more likely to have the energy and resilience needed to consistently provide high-quality care. Burnout, on the other hand, can leave you feeling drained, both physically and emotionally, making it challenging to meet the demands of caregiving effectively.

Secondly, a healthy mental state is vital for maintaining focus and attention to even the most routine caregiving tasks. When your mental health is compromised, your capacity to concentrate diminishes, increasing the risk of making errors with potentially severe consequences. This could range from administering incorrect medications to missing crucial doctor's appointments, all of which can pose a significant threat to your loved one's well-being.

Neglecting your mental health can also make you less equipped to cope with the inherent stress of being a caregiver. Prolonged stress and untreated mental health issues may lead to depression, ultimately resulting in poor decision-making. For instance, a study in the U.S. involving hospice and palliative social workers identified caregivers at risk of suicide. Shockingly, over half of them reported warning signs of suicide, and a significant number reported actual suicide attempts or deaths. These distressing statistics underscore the severe consequences that can arise when mental health is overlooked.

Regrettably, there are heart-wrenching cases of loving and devoted parents who, in the grip of severe depression or other mental illnesses, have attempted to harm their disabled children, and tragically, some have succeeded in ending their own lives as well. The stories of individuals like Frank Stack, who took the lives of his intellectually challenged children and wife, or Bonnie Liltz, who tragically ended her daughter's life and attempted suicide, serve as painful reminders of the dire outcomes that can result from untreated mental health issues.

However, there are also instances, like that of Yvette Nichol, where intervention and support led to a brighter outcome. Yvette, who faced a period of depression, attempted to harm her disabled son and herself, but both survived. Such cases underscore the importance of addressing mental health proactively and seeking assistance when needed.

These heartrending scenarios not only emphasize the critical importance of safeguarding your mental health as a caregiver but also serve as a stark reminder that when our mental well-being falters, our actions can inadvertently harm our loved ones.

Furthermore, it's essential to recognize that your mental health has a direct impact on your physical health. High-stress levels, for instance, can lead to increased inflammation throughout the body and contribute to conditions like elevated blood pressure, which can subsequently lead to more severe health issues such as coronary artery disease and heart attacks. Therefore, protecting your mental health should not be a reactive measure but a proactive and ongoing commitment.

In conclusion, prioritizing your mental health as a caregiver is not just about self-care; it's about ensuring the safety, well-being, and quality of care you provide to your loved one. It's a crucial step in preventing burnout, avoiding serious mistakes, and safeguarding against the severe consequences that can arise from untreated mental health issues. Moreover, your physical health is closely linked to your mental well-being, making it all the more vital to maintain good mental health consistently.

At what point should I become concerned about my mental well-being?

Experiencing occasional stress, anxiety, or even periods of low mood is a normal part of the human experience. After all, as humans, we are not exempt from life's trials and tribulations, which can test our emotional resilience.

---

[10] Dwyer, S., Janssens, A., Sansom, A., Biddle, L., Mars, B., Slater, T., Moran, P., Stallard, P., Melluish, J., Reakes, L., Walker, A., Andrewartha, C. and Hastings, R., 2021. Suicidality in family caregivers of people with long-term illnesses and disabilities: A scoping review. Comprehensive

However, the point at which concern arises is when these emotions become so overwhelming that they disrupt our ability to carry out daily tasks or derive enjoyment from life.

At this juncture, it may signal the presence of a mental health issue that requires professional intervention to help us regain our equilibrium.

Let's embark on a brief self-assessment, using the table provided below, to gauge the current state of our mental health and determine whether it warrants further attention and support.

Symptom	Frequency			
	Never	Rarely	Occasionally	Often
	(I've never felt this way)	(I've experienced this symptom in the past, but it feels like eons since the last occurrence.)	(I've experienced this on a few occasions, but they've been quite infrequent.)	(Yes, I get this frequently)
Feeling hopeless about the future				
Withdrawing from friends and activities that used to give you joy				
Feeling overwhelmed by your responsibilities				
Feeling restless or agitated most of the time				
Experiencing persistent sadness, worry, or anger				
Experiencing a sudden change in appetite or				

Psychiatry, 110, p.152261

weight					
Sleeping too much or too little					
You are using drugs or alcohol to cope					
Thinking about harming yourself or someone else					
You are constantly tired and run down					

If your answers to the questions above consistently fell in the "Never" category, let me extend my heartfelt congratulations. You're not only an outstanding parent, but you also exemplify the pinnacle of mental well-being. Your experience serves as a shining testament that even in this wonderfully imperfect world, true perfection can, indeed, be attained.

On the other hand, if most of your responses fell in the "rarely" category or you often chose "occasionally," you're perfectly in line with the majority of individuals. It's a sign that you're likely doing well in managing your mental health.

However, if you noticed that your answers frequently landed on "often" or "always" for most of the questions, this could be an indicator that your mental health is not currently in the optimal state. In such a case, seeking assistance may be a wise decision to guide you back from the red zone and towards a healthier mental well-being.

What Steps Can I Take to Improve My Situation?

If you're concerned about the state of your mental health, don't be afraid. You're not alone in this experience, as mental health challenges are surprisingly common. It's perfectly okay to acknowledge that you might be going through a tough time. The good news is that help and support are available, and with time, patience, and some effort, you can navigate your struggles and put them behind you.

Now, let's delve into how you can proactively enhance your mental health.

To start, prioritize getting adequate sleep and rest. Sufficient sleep allows for clearer thinking and better decision-making regarding your child's future. Sleeping in a cool environment can significantly improve the quality of your rest, so it's worth exploring ways to stay cool and comfortable during the night.

Openness in delegating tasks to others can free up time for much-needed rest. For example, asking a helpful neighbor to assist with grocery shopping can give you precious moments to relax, take a short nap, or simply enjoy a quiet moment.

Maintaining a balanced and nutritious diet is another key factor in boosting your mental health. Nutrient-rich foods can positively impact your mood and provide increased energy. A healthy diet is also vital for those recovering from substance abuse.

On the topic of substance use, reducing or eliminating alcohol and other intoxicating substances can be instrumental in maintaining a clear mind and making sound decisions. Abstaining entirely from such substances may prove to be the wisest long-term choice, as even moderate use can escalate over time.

Regular physical activity is crucial for preserving mental health. Exercise releases endorphins, which are natural mood enhancers and stress reducers. Engaging in low-impact sports like ping pong or joining a gym can be beneficial, but even a simple activity like walking in the park can work wonders. If your child has mobility limitations, consider water-based exercise with appropriate safety measures.

Surrounding yourself with positive and optimistic individuals who encourage a brighter outlook on life is essential. Positive people often consciously distance themselves from negativity, so try to avoid consistently adopting a pessimistic perspective. Focusing on the positive side of life can be aided by creating a "Gratitude Wall" in your home, where you document the best aspects of each day, week, or month to maintain a positive mindset.

Dedicate time to activities that bring you joy and reduce stress. Engaging in hobbies like reading, gardening, or listening to music can boost satisfaction and overall mental well-being. Exploring relaxation techniques such as yoga, meditation, or deep breathing exercises can also be highly effective.

If you're struggling to manage your mental health, seeking professional assistance is paramount. Numerous helplines and support groups are available to provide guidance and support. Additionally, consult with your healthcare provider who can offer information about available treatments and medications.

By following these recommendations, you'll be well on your way to improving your mental health. Remember, even if you're an "Übermensch" or simply like most people, safeguarding your mental well-being is a crucial task. So, taking the steps mentioned above is a positive and proactive choice for everyone.

How Can I Seek Assistance Without Neglecting My Child's Needs?

Recognizing your concerns about caring for your child, especially when your own well-being is in question, is entirely natural. Your child depends on you, and your presence is vital.

First and foremost, there's no need to distance yourself from your child unless the situation absolutely demands it. You can include them in your enjoyable activities, exercise routines, and other adventures. The only scenario in which your physical absence might be necessary is when you're seeking therapy.

Nevertheless, being temporarily unavailable doesn't equate to abandonment if you have a well-structured plan in place. To navigate this situation effectively, you should establish a caregiving network for your child. This network could include your spouse, other family members, or close friends—people you can trust to assist you when needed.

Having a caregiving network is crucial for various reasons. It ensures that your child's life and well-being don't revolve solely around you. It also means that you can introduce your child to other sources of care. This can help your child become accustomed to your absence, benefiting both their adaptability and your own mental health.

Over time, your child can develop a sense of security in the knowledge that there are reliable caregivers available besides you. This not only allows you to take breaks when needed but also prepares your child for a future in which they may need alternate caregivers, even after you're no longer able to provide care.

If, for any reason, you can't establish a caregiving network among friends and relatives, you can explore respite care as an option for brief periods of relief. To make any potential future breaks smoother for your child, it's helpful to start introducing caregivers into their routine as early as possible. For instance, you might have a home health aide visit a few days a week to gradually acquaint your child with the idea.

Remember, you shouldn't restrict your options just to avoid being away from your child. Unless you're deemed a severe risk to yourself or others, extended hospitalization for mental therapy is unlikely.

The earlier you seek help, the better your chances of recovery and returning to your life and your child. If you find yourself struggling to cope, understand that this isn't the end of the road; there is assistance available to guide you through this phase. Seeking professional help doesn't mean you're endangering your child; it's a decision that could quite literally save your life and theirs. Don't hesitate to seek professional assistance, even if it means being temporarily away. It could be a life-saving choice.

SIX

WHEN I AM GONE

When I am no longer here, what choices are available to ensure the well-being of my adult child with disabilities?

When contemplating the future and the well-being of your adult child with disabilities after you're no longer here, it's understandable that you may feel a sense of unease. While thoughts of mortality are often uncomfortable, as a parent in this unique situation, your concerns are entirely valid. The passage of time and witnessing the illness or passing of loved ones can further intensify these worries. As the primary caregiver for your child, it's only natural to wonder about their future and how their needs will be met in your absence.

Fortunately, there are options available for parents of disabled adults to ensure their child's ongoing care and support even after they have passed away. Although contemplating and planning for this scenario may be emotionally challenging, it provides a sense of comfort and security, knowing that your child will continue to be cared for. Moreover, involving your child in the planning process and considering their input can make the transition smoother and provide them with a greater sense of empowerment.

Here are some options to consider:

1. Special Needs Trust: Establishing a special needs trust is a popular and effective method for safeguarding your child's financial future. This trust allows you to set aside funds and assets for their benefit, while still ensuring their eligibility for government benefits, such as Medicaid and Supplemental Security Income (SSI). Working with an attorney experienced in special needs planning can help you navigate the complexities of creating and managing a special needs trust.

2. Guardianship: Selecting a guardian for your adult child with disabilities is a crucial decision to make. The guardian will assume the responsibility of providing care, making important decisions, and advocating for your child's well-being. Identifying a trustworthy and capable guardian who understands your child's needs and shares your values is essential.

3. Future Housing Options: Explore housing alternatives that cater specifically to individuals with disabilities. Group homes supported living arrangements, or specialized housing communities can provide a supportive environment where your child's needs are met, and they can thrive independently. Research local organizations, agencies, and resources that offer housing options and support services for individuals with disabilities.

4. Caregiver and Support Network: Identify and establish a network of caregivers and supportive individuals who can assist in caring for your adult child. This network can include relatives, close friends, community organizations, or professionals experienced in working with individuals with disabilities. Ensuring that your child has a reliable support system in place will contribute to their well-being and quality of life.

5. Documenting Instructions and Preferences: Prepare comprehensive documentation outlining your child's preferences, routines, medical history, and any specific instructions that will assist caregivers in understanding their unique needs. This documentation should be easily accessible and regularly updated to reflect any changes in your child's circumstances or preferences.

Seeking professional guidance from attorneys specializing in estate planning, disability law, and special needs planning is invaluable during this process. They can provide legal advice tailored to your specific situation and help you navigate the complexities of ensuring a secure future for your adult child with disabilities.

Although contemplating and planning for a future without your physical presence can be emotionally challenging, taking these proactive steps brings peace of mind and ensures that your child's well-being and care continue in a manner that aligns with your wishes. By addressing these concerns head-on and involving your child in the planning process, you can rest easier knowing that their future is secure and that they will receive the support and care they deserve.

Institutes and Facilities

When you think of "institutions and facilities," it's essential to recognize that the standards and paradigms for care have significantly evolved. Long gone are the days of custodial care; contemporary care emphasizes dignity, choice, and individuality.

In the past, residents were often grouped together in dormitories with minimal control over their lives, including their time, energy, and resources. Today, residents frequently participate in the management of their care and advocate for improved living standards while maintaining affordability.

These institutes and facilities are intentionally designed to provide specialized care for individuals with disabilities. The staff typically possesses extensive experience and specialized knowledge to cater to the residents' specific needs. These facilities are well-resourced and offer access to a wide range of services and activities, ensuring a high quality of life.

Let's explore some noteworthy options in this evolving landscape.

Group Homes

Group homes provide a communal living environment that closely resembles everyday home life. Often, they house adults with similar disabilities who are cared for by a team of dedicated staff.

Group homes can be privately operated for-profit businesses, nonprofit organizations, or government-run facilities. They typically maintain a smaller staff-to-resident ratio than nursing homes and prioritize individualized support with daily activities.

What's remarkable about group homes is that they are usually integrated within local communities and outwardly resemble regular houses, making the institutionalized feeling a non-issue. While one-on-one care staff time may be limited compared to live-in caregivers, group homes offer the advantage of round-the-clock supervision. Residents can receive essential training, assistance, and therapeutic services.

Moreover, group homes provide a wide array of activities and opportunities for socialization, such as crafts and field trips.

This is especially important for disabled adults who might face challenges engaging in social interactions. They also facilitate transportation for medical appointments and recreational outings.

Group homes tend to cater to individuals with similar disabilities, allowing for more disability-specific services and home modifications. The staff's extensive experience in serving residents with disabilities is a significant advantage.

Living in a group home fosters social interaction and a sense of belonging among residents. Furthermore, group homes strike a balance between privacy and social interaction. Residents have their bedrooms while sharing communal spaces like the kitchen, living room, and bathrooms. This balance offers structure and routine, which can be beneficial for disabled adults who may struggle with impulsivity or disorganization.

By providing stability and continuity, group homes help residents transition to a life with less upheaval after the loss of parental care. It's essential to note that while group homes may not always accommodate individuals with more severe disabilities or complex medical conditions, they can often collaborate with specialized providers to supplement care.

Assisted Living Facilities

Assisted living facilities offer various housing options and assistance with daily living activities for disabled adults. These facilities can include apartments, shared dwellings, and separate one-floor homes within a larger community.

Compared to group homes, assisted living facilities can accommodate a more extensive and diverse population. The level of independence is higher, and the resident-to-staff ratio is lower. These facilities usually cater to 33 or more residents, offering a more independent environment. [2]

Unlike group homes, assisted living facilities don't focus on a specific disability type. The choice of an assisted living facility depends on your child's level of care needs. If your child can't manage some activities of daily living independently but is otherwise self-sufficient, this may be a suitable option.

It's important to note that the quality of care in assisted living facilities can vary widely.

To ensure the facility meets your expectations, consider visiting unannounced to observe the environment and staff-resident interactions. Research the facility's policies, services, and recreational amenities.

Moreover, inquire about the facility's plan for the transition to more intensive care, especially if your child's needs change over time. Location is also a crucial factor. Ensure the facility is accessible to guardians and support networks for check-ins and emergencies. 3

The facility's proximity to potential work opportunities should be considered as well, as employment prospects may be a part of your child's future. Particularly relevant in light of the recent pandemic, assess the facility's infection control procedures to protect residents from infectious diseases. 4

Ultimately, your child's needs and preferences are paramount. Involve them in the decision-making process to ensure their comfort and satisfaction with the chosen facility. These considerations collectively help determine the most suitable option for your child's care and well-being.

Nursing Homes

While nursing homes serve as a crucial care option for many, it's important to acknowledge that they may not always align with the needs of every disabled adult. However, nursing homes can be an optimal solution when dealing with individuals facing chronic illnesses or disabilities demanding round-the-clock skilled nursing care and supervision.

In some cases, disabilities are chronic and degenerative, exhibiting a progressive worsening over time. Under such circumstances, group homes and assisted living facilities may fall short in providing the comprehensive medical care and support required. Nursing homes have become the preferred choice to ensure the well-being and specialized care for these individuals.

It's worth noting that nursing homes predominantly serve a senior population, constituting a substantial portion of the facility's residents. This demographic characteristic can influence the dynamics within these homes, including the staffing, social activities, and overall atmosphere. Consequently, the environment in nursing homes may not always be well-suited for younger disabled adults.

For parents considering a nursing home as the best option for their child, it's advisable to seek facilities that specialize in caring for people with disabilities or maintain dedicated wings or floors for younger residents.

Furthermore, an exploration of the facility's capabilities and expertise in treating the child's specific disability is essential for making an informed decision.

Beyond medical services, the availability of adequate socialization initiatives should also be a key consideration. Given that these places will become your child's long-term residence, ensuring their happiness and comfort is of paramount importance.

Adult Foster Care (AFC) Homes

Defining an AFC home can be somewhat flexible as these definitions tend to vary by state. Nonetheless, they commonly involve providing non-medical care to a small group of disabled or elderly adults, often limited to one to six individuals. Adult foster care homes share notable similarities with group homes and assisted living facilities.

One standout advantage of AFC homes over other assisted living facilities is their potential for more personalized attention due to their smaller resident populations. However, it's essential to recognize that unless they are specialized foster homes, residents in most adult foster homes might not receive the same level of disability-specific care that a group home is likely to provide.

A significant distinction between adult foster care and assisted living is the presence of awake workers. AFC homes offer 24-hour assistance, but staff members are not mandated to remain awake at all times; their presence is required as needed. In contrast, assisted living facilities maintain a continuous, round-the-clock awake staff.

AFC homes offer a more cost-effective alternative to aging in place, as they are often established in existing single-family apartments. Caregivers bear the majority of capital expenditures, including mortgage payments, home alterations, and repairs, while government costs are primarily limited to providing financial support for eligible individuals. Additionally, AFC caregivers often deliver lower-level, and therefore less expensive, services compared to nursing institution caregivers. [11]

---

[11] 7Donna Dosman and Norah Keating, "Cheaper for Whom? Costs Experienced by Formal Caregivers in Adult
Family Living Programs", Journal of Aging & Social Policy 17.2 (2005): 67-83, online, Internet, 21 Sep. 2022. . 8"Adult Foster Care: How It Works, Financial Assistance & Payment Options", Payingforseniorcare.com, 2020, online, Internet, 16 Sep. 2022. , Available: https://www.payingforseniorcare.com/adult-foster-care. 9Independentfutures.com, 2022, online,

Although Medicare benefits typically do not cover home and board-related fees, they can assist with the "care-related" components of the charges incurred. These insights are vital when considering the most suitable care setting for your child's unique needs.

Housing opportunities for persons with disabilities

Housing opportunities for persons with disabilities are essential to ensure inclusivity, independence, and a high quality of life. Various housing options and programs are available to support individuals with disabilities in finding suitable and accessible homes. Here are some key housing opportunities for persons with disabilities:

1. Accessible Housing: Accessible housing refers to homes specifically designed or modified to accommodate individuals with disabilities. These homes typically have features such as wheelchair ramps, widened doorways, roll-in showers, and grab bars. Accessible housing allows individuals with disabilities to navigate their living spaces more easily and promotes independence.

2. Supportive Housing: Supportive housing provides a combination of affordable housing and support services tailored to meet the needs of individuals with disabilities. These services may include personal care assistance, counseling, life skills training, and access to healthcare. Supportive housing aims to help individuals with disabilities live as independently as possible while receiving the necessary support to thrive.

3. Group Homes: Group homes, also known as residential care facilities, are shared living arrangements where individuals with disabilities live together and receive support from trained staff. Group homes provide a supportive environment where residents can develop social connections and access assistance with daily activities, such as meal preparation, medication management, and personal care.

4. Independent Living Apartments: Independent living apartments are private units designed for individuals with disabilities who desire a greater level of autonomy and independence. These apartments offer accessibility features and may be located within communities that provide supportive services and amenities, such as transportation, social activities, and access to

---

Internet, 21 Sep. 2022. , Available: https://independentfutures.com/wp content/uploads/2018/06/EnglishHousingGuide-min.pdf.

healthcare.

5. Section 8 Housing Choice Vouchers: The Section 8 Housing Choice Voucher program, administered by the U.S. Department of Housing and Urban Development (HUD), provides rental assistance to eligible low-income individuals, including those with disabilities. Voucher recipients can choose housing in the private market, and the program subsidizes a portion of their rent.

6. Nonprofit Housing Organizations: Numerous nonprofit organizations focus on developing and managing housing options for individuals with disabilities. These organizations work to provide affordable, accessible, and supportive housing. Examples include L'Arche International, Mercy Housing, and Accessible Space Inc.

7. Home Modification Programs: Some government agencies and nonprofit organizations offer home modification programs that provide financial assistance for necessary adaptations to make existing homes accessible. These modifications can include installing ramps, widening doorways, adding grab bars, or lowering countertops. These programs aim to enable individuals with disabilities to age in place and live safely in their homes.

8. Fair Housing Rights: It's crucial for individuals with disabilities to be aware of their fair housing rights. The Fair Housing Act prohibits discrimination based on disability and ensures equal access to housing opportunities. If faced with discrimination or accessibility barriers in housing, individuals can file complaints with HUD or local fair housing organizations.

When seeking housing opportunities for persons with disabilities, it's advisable to connect with local disability advocacy groups, housing authorities, and social service agencies. These organizations can provide information on available housing options, application processes, and financial assistance programs specific to the local area.

Ultimately, ensuring accessible and suitable housing options for persons with disabilities is a vital aspect of fostering inclusivity and promoting their overall well-being and independence.

Integrated Community Living

Integrated community living represents a progressive and heartwarming living option that numerous families are actively embracing. This innovative approach capitalizes on collaborative partnerships between families, each caring for disabled members, to construct an inclusive community designed to flourish and provide lifelong support for their children, even beyond the parents' lifetimes.

The mechanism is simple yet profound: participating families come together to create living spaces within a designated community. These homes are specially adapted to meet the specific needs of their disabled children or siblings, fostering an environment that promotes independence while nurturing close-knit relationships within the community.

Integrated community living achieves multiple critical goals. Foremost, it ensures that disabled adults are perpetually embedded in a support network, enjoying companionship, and social interaction with both disabled and non-disabled individuals. This interconnectedness is facilitated by an environment that prioritizes accessibility for all disabled community members, and the provision of essential services, such as healthcare clinics and accessible transportation, tailored to their unique needs.

What makes these communities exceptional is their capacity to forge alternative societal structures. A notable example is the establishment of a Timebank within the community. Here, community members contribute their time and skills to take care of one another, earning "time credits" that can be utilized when they or their loved ones require assistance. In this symbiotic exchange, residents are not only ensuring their child's well-being but also engaging in a dynamic web of care and interdependence.

The critical takeaway is that while integrated community living presents a promising vision for care and support, it should not be viewed as a utopian solution. Like any other society, these communities have their limitations. Therefore, it is essential to have comprehensive plans in place to address the child's specific needs. For instance, while support for a relatively independent individual may be readily available, more complex, or constant care requirements may necessitate exploring the additional options discussed above. These plans should be clearly communicated and coordinated with potential caregivers well in advance.

Complementary Care Options

Effective planning encompasses more than securing living arrangements. It should encompass the broader spectrum of your child's needs, including their financial and spiritual well-being.

Empowering your child with vocational skills remains a crucial aspect. Organizations like OWL, RNIB, EARN, Scope, Ability Jobs, Source America, Equally Able, and others can be invaluable for fostering skill development and employment opportunities. Consider locating vocational agencies near your child's planned living arrangement to ensure they can access these vital services.

Exploring government job opportunities can also be beneficial, as they might grant access to additional benefits that contribute to your child's care. It's essential to investigate these opportunities, assess their eligibility criteria, and navigate the application process to secure your child's future.

In acknowledging your child's spiritual needs, consider engaging with your faith community to ensure continued support after you're gone. Discuss your wishes with your religious leader or clergy to facilitate a seamless transition for your child's spiritual practice. Many organizations, such as the National Catholic Partnership on Disability, AAIDD, Religion and Spirituality Division, Friendship Ministries, Walk Right In Ministries, MUHSEN, Enabled Muslim, and others, offer religious services designed for disabled individuals.

Additionally, emotional needs should not be overlooked. Designate a responsible individual who can provide love and support, serving as a mentor and a confidant for your child. This individual may not necessarily be the child's legal guardian but should have a positive and close relationship with your child, an understanding of their unique needs, and the time and patience to provide the necessary support. This person may be a close friend, a family member, or even a case worker from your child's support network.

Baby Boomer Trend-Proactive Housing

A current trend among baby boomers is the independent investment in homes that are converted to create group homes for their adult children with disabilities to live in after the parents pass away. This emerging approach reflects a proactive and forward-thinking mindset among baby boomers who want to ensure the well-being and long-term housing stability of their children with disabilities.

The motivation behind this trend stems from a desire to provide a nurturing and supportive environment for their adult children, even when the parents are no longer able to provide direct care. By converting their own homes or investing in suitable properties, baby boomers are taking steps to establish long-term housing solutions tailored to the unique needs of their children with disabilities.

There are several key factors contributing to the popularity of this trend:

1. Personalized Care and Support: Baby boomers recognize the importance of personalized care and support for their adult children with disabilities. By establishing group homes, they can ensure that their children receive specialized care and assistance from trained staff, while also fostering a sense of community and social interaction among the residents.

2. Continuity and Stability: Creating group homes allows baby boomers to maintain a sense of continuity and stability in the lives of their adult children with disabilities. By investing in properties and establishing legal frameworks, such as trusts or nonprofit organizations, they can ensure that the group homes will continue to operate and provide housing for their children even after they pass away.

3. Collaboration and Shared Responsibility: The establishment of group homes encourages collaboration and shared responsibility among family members, siblings, and the broader community. Baby boomers often involve their other children and relatives in the planning and management of the group homes, ensuring a support network is in place to sustain the housing model in the long term.

4. Customized Adaptations and Accessibility: Converting homes specifically for group living allows baby boomers to customize the physical environment to meet the unique accessibility needs of their adult children with disabilities. Modifications can include wheelchair accessibility, sensory adaptations, safety features, and communal spaces designed for social interaction and inclusivity.

To proceed with this trend, baby boomers typically engage in the following steps:

1. Financial Planning: Baby boomers assess their financial situation and explore funding options to acquire or modify properties for group home conversion. This may involve utilizing personal savings, considering home equity options, or seeking financial assistance from government programs, grants, or nonprofit organizations.

2. Legal Considerations: Seeking legal advice is crucial to ensure proper estate planning and the establishment of appropriate legal frameworks, such as trusts or nonprofit entities, to oversee the operation of the group homes after the parents' passing. This helps ensure continuity, financial stability, and adherence to relevant regulations.

3. Collaboration and Partnerships: Baby boomers engage in discussions with family members, potential caregivers, and community organizations to build a network of support and determine the roles and responsibilities of various stakeholders involved in the group home initiative.

4. Property Conversion and Adaptation: Homes are converted or modified to accommodate the needs of individuals with disabilities. This may involve architectural renovations, accessibility modifications, and the installation of appropriate equipment and assistive devices.

5. Staffing and Caregiver Selection: Baby boomers carefully select and train qualified staff and caregivers who will provide the necessary support and care for their adult children with disabilities. Screening, interviews, and background checks are typically conducted to ensure the individuals entrusted with caregiving responsibilities are well-suited for the role.

It's important to note that while this trend highlights the proactive efforts of baby boomers to address the housing needs of their adult children with disabilities, it may not be feasible or appropriate for every family. The decision to establish group homes should be made after thorough consideration of individual circumstances, financial resources, local regulations, and the availability of suitable support networks.

Overall, the trend of baby boomers independently investing in homes converted to create group homes for their adult children with disabilities reflects a growing commitment to long-term housing solutions and the well-being of their loved ones. By taking proactive measures, baby boomers are leaving a lasting legacy of care, support, and independence for their children with disabilities.

The Future of Housing

As of our last research update in September 2021, there were several emerging trends and advancements in proactive housing for people with disabilities. While we cannot provide information on developments beyond 2021, we can outline some of the promising directions and possibilities that could have continued evolving in this field as of 2024 and beyond:

1. **Universal Design and Accessibility**: Universal design principles, which focus on creating environments accessible to all, were becoming more prominent in architecture and housing construction. The integration of features like ramps, wider doorways, smart home technologies, and voice-activated controls in housing could have become even more widespread.

2. **Innovative Technology**: The adoption of smart home technology was poised to make homes more adaptive and responsive to individual needs. Advances in artificial intelligence (AI) and the Internet of Things (IoT) might have led to further developments, such as predictive technology that anticipates a person's needs.

3. **Personalized and Adaptable Spaces**: Housing design aimed to provide flexible spaces that could be easily adapted to accommodate the changing needs of individuals with disabilities. Modular and movable walls, furniture, and fixtures could provide a customized living environment.

4. **Co-Living and Community Initiatives**: Collaborative housing models, such as co-living communities, were gaining attention. These communities emphasize shared spaces and resources, which can be especially beneficial for individuals with disabilities by providing a built-in support network.

5. **Sustainability and Energy Efficiency**: An increasing focus on eco-friendly and energy-efficient housing could have also extended to accessible housing. The use of sustainable materials, energy-efficient appliances, and solar panels could make housing more cost-effective and environmentally friendly.

6. **Virtual Reality and Augmented Reality**: Advances in virtual reality (VR) and augmented reality (AR) technologies might enable architects and designers to create and test accessible living spaces in a virtual environment. This could help in optimizing layouts and designs for people with various disabilities.

7. **Government Initiatives**: Public policies and incentives aimed at promoting accessible housing could have continued to evolve. Governments may have introduced regulations and incentives to encourage universal design features in all new housing projects.

8. **Supportive Services**: The integration of support services within housing complexes was on the rise. In addition to accessible physical spaces, this includes on-site caregiving, health services, and access to social and

recreational activities.

9. **Online Platforms for Housing Search**: Digital platforms and applications for finding accessible housing were becoming more common. Such platforms facilitate the search for housing that meets specific accessibility requirements.

10. **Consumer Input**: The involvement of people with disabilities and their families in the design and planning of housing continued to be a crucial trend. Their feedback and input help ensure that housing solutions are genuinely tailored to their needs.

Please note that developments in housing often depend on regional policies, regulations, and economic conditions. To get the most up-to-date information on advancements in proactive housing for people with disabilities and their families in 2024 and beyond, we recommend consulting recent publications, government agencies, and organizations focused on disability rights and accessibility.

Conclusion

In conclusion, it's paramount to recognize that your passing doesn't signify the end of the road for your child. They can indeed continue to receive excellent care and lead a happy and fulfilling life. Instead of dwelling on pessimistic thoughts regarding your child's future, it's crucial to proactively embark on creating a plan that ensures their well-being and happiness long after you're gone.

Understanding the array of options available for securing your child's future is the simple part; the real challenge lies in crafting a comprehensive plan. Fortunately, you don't have to undertake this journey alone. Numerous initiatives and organizations are dedicated to providing assistance and guidance throughout this process.

For instance, consider resources like The Arc's Future Planning Project or The Academy of Special Needs Planners. These initiatives can offer invaluable support and expertise in charting a course for your child's future. By tapping into these resources, you'll find yourself surrounded by a community of individuals and organizations dedicated to helping you build a secure and hopeful future for your child.

So, take heart and understand that you're not alone in this endeavor. Countless individuals and organizations stand ready to aid you in planning for your child's future. With their assistance, you can take the steps needed to ensure that your child's life remains vibrant and promising, even after you've moved on. This, my friend, is more than sufficient reason to hold on to hope.

SEVEN

HOW TO PREPARE FOR UNFORESEEN CIRCUMSTANCES WHILE I'M STILL PRESENT

Imagine you're a ship captain, commanding your vessel across the open sea. Out of the blue, your radio crackles to life, and a voice on the other end warns of an unforeseen storm lurking directly in your path, with no chance to retreat. What's your course of action in this precarious situation? Do you passively hope for better weather, taking a gamble with the safety of your crew and ship? Maybe you resign yourself to fate, singing "Que Sera Sera" while awaiting the storm's fury to pass? Or do you seize the helm, adjust the sails, and take proactive measures to navigate the tempest safely?

By this stage in life, you've likely come to terms with the fact that our journey isn't always smooth sailing on tranquil waters. Storms, both literal and metaphorical, can materialize swiftly, catching us off-guard. While we can't foresee every curveball life hurls our way, we can certainly take steps to fortify ourselves for any tempest that may arise, especially as we age, and our reserves of energy and resources become more limited.

Understanding the Significance of Preparing for the Unforeseen

As we advance in years, the significance of preparing for the unforeseen becomes increasingly apparent. This preparation involves crafting a robust plan for those moments when things take an unexpected turn. This becomes even more critical for elderly parents with disabled adult children, as they might lack the same support structures available to other seniors. Moreover, they can't solely rely on their physical and mental abilities to navigate through unforeseen crises.

A multitude of unforeseen events can unfold, frequently revolving around accidents, financial challenges, and unexpected medical requirements. This chapter will delve into how elderly parents of disabled adults can methodically prepare for the unexpected and lay the groundwork to respond to emergencies effectively.

Accidents and Preparedness for Emergencies

The mere thought of accidents is something most of us prefer to brush aside, yet the reality is that they can occur unexpectedly, taking on various shapes and sizes. From minor mishaps, like a scraped knee, to more severe incidents such as broken bones, the spectrum of accidents is broad. While many accidents aren't life-threatening, it's vital to acknowledge that some hold the potential to be just that. Hence, it's imperative to have a well-thought-out plan in place to handle them.

This section explores strategies to prepare for accidents:

Implementing Fall Prevention Measures

Falls represent one of the primary causes of injuries among seniors, with a significant percentage of adults aged 60 and above reporting falls each year. In developed countries like the United States, these falls account for up to 75% of elderly injuries and are a leading cause of hospitalization.

As such, it's paramount to proactively address fall prevention. A few straightforward fall prevention strategies include:

1. **Enhanced Lighting**: Properly illuminating your living spaces can substantially reduce the risk of accidental falls. Well-lit areas enhance visibility and make navigation safer.

2. **Hazard Removal**: Identifying and removing tripping hazards throughout your home is crucial. This can entail securing loose rugs, organizing clutter, and ensuring that pathways are free from obstructions.

3. **Appropriate Footwear**: Choosing suitable footwear is often underestimated. Comfortable and supportive shoes can significantly contribute to fall prevention.

4. **Assistive Devices**: If necessary, employ assistive devices such as canes or walkers. These tools provide added stability and support, reducing the

likelihood of accidents.[12]

5. **Exercise Routine**: Engaging in regular physical activity can improve strength and balance, making individuals more resilient to accidents. Consider incorporating exercises tailored to enhancing these specific attributes.

Harnessing the Power of Smart Home Devices

While smart home devices are commonly associated with convenience and luxury, they also play a vital role in safeguarding against accidents. These innovative devices offer various ways to protect both you and your child from unexpected incidents. Here are a few examples:

1. **Motion-Activated Lighting**: Beyond their utility in deterring potential intruders, motion sensor-activated lights also serve as excellent safety features. They can prevent accidents by illuminating dark areas, ensuring safe navigation within your home.

2. **Smart Thermostats:** Smart thermostats contribute to safety by promoting energy efficiency and reducing fire risks. These devices can automatically adjust temperature settings when they detect that a room is unoccupied, mitigating the potential for accidents related to overheating or electrical faults.

By proactively implementing these measures and embracing the possibilities offered by smart home technology, you can significantly enhance accident prevention and preparedness, ultimately creating a safer environment for both you and your child.

Connected smoke detectors serve as a critical component of your home's safety infrastructure. These innovative devices offer more than just traditional smoke detection; they can provide an early warning system that is indispensable in the event of a fire. Here's how connected smoke detectors work and why they are invaluable:

---

[12] 1Curtis S. Florence et al., "Medical Costs of Fatal and Nonfatal Falls in Older Adults", Journal of the American Geriatrics Society 66.4 (2018): 693-698, online, Internet, 16 Sep. 2022. , Available: https://www.ncbi.nlm.nih.gov/pmc/articles/PMC6089380/#R1. 2J A Stevens et al., "The costs of fatal and non-fatal falls among older adults", Injury Prevention 12.5 (2006): 290-295, online, Internet, 22 Sep. 2022, Available: https://www.ncbi.nlm.nih.gov/pmc/articles/PMC2563445/. 3"Fall prevention: Simple tips to prevent falls", Mayo Clinic, 2022, online, Internet, 26 Sep. 2022. Available: https://www.mayoclinic.org/healthy-lifestyle/healthy-aging/in-depth/fall-prevention/art 20047358.

1. **Advanced Sensing Technology**: Connected smoke detectors are equipped with state-of-the-art sensing technology that can swiftly detect even the smallest traces of smoke or rising temperatures. This sensitivity ensures that potential fire hazards are identified at the earliest stages.

2. **Real-Time Alerts**: When smoke or heat anomalies are detected, these detectors trigger real-time alerts. These alerts are usually transmitted to your smartphone or other connected devices, ensuring that you are immediately informed of the situation, no matter where you are.

3. **Valuable Time Gained**: In the event of a fire, every second counts. Connected smoke detectors provide you with precious additional time to take action. This time could be the difference between a controlled evacuation and a dangerous situation.

4. **Remote Monitoring**: Many of these detectors offer remote monitoring capabilities. This means you can check on your home's safety status from afar. If you are away from home and receive an alert, you can contact emergency services or neighbors to respond promptly.

5. **Integration with Home Security**: Connected smoke detectors often integrate seamlessly with your home security system. In the event of a fire, the system can automatically alert both the local fire department and you, expediting emergency response.

6. **Testing and Maintenance**: These detectors usually offer self-testing features and maintenance alerts. They can notify you when it's time to replace the batteries or if there are any malfunctions. This ensures that your smoke detection system remains in optimal working condition.

7. **Reduced False Alarms**: Advanced technology in these detectors helps reduce false alarms. They can distinguish between harmless cooking smoke and a real fire, reducing the inconvenience of unnecessary alarms.

In conclusion, connected smoke detectors are not just fire alarms; they are a vital safety net for your home. By providing early warnings and real-time alerts, they offer the critical advantage of time in the event of a fire, enabling you and your family to evacuate safely. Furthermore, their integration with home security systems and remote monitoring capabilities makes them an indispensable tool in modern home safety.

Prepare for the Unexpected: Managing Financial Emergencies

No one likes to dwell on the possibility of financial emergencies, yet they can strike without warning and in various forms. Whether it's an unforeseen medical expense, a sudden job loss, or an urgent car repair, being financially prepared for these contingencies is essential, especially for older adults. This section outlines effective strategies to safeguard your financial well-being and ensure you're ready to handle any financial curveballs life might throw at you.

1. **Build an Emergency Fund**

Having an emergency fund is your financial safety net. It's a sum of money set aside explicitly to cover unforeseen expenses. Begin with a goal of saving at least $1,000, but ideally aim to accumulate an amount equal to 3-6 months of living expenses. Your emergency fund acts as a cushion, helping you avoid debt when sudden financial needs arise.

2. **Make a Budget**

Budgeting is a valuable tool for tracking your spending and ensuring you don't live beyond your means. It also enables you to allocate funds for your emergency fund. Minor adjustments to your budget, such as dining out less frequently or cutting back on entertainment expenses, can significantly boost your ability to save for financial emergencies.

3. **Invest in Insurance**

Insurance plays a vital role in protecting your financial health. Health, life, and homeowners' insurance can cover the costs of unexpected medical bills, car repairs, and other unforeseen expenses. While insurance can't prevent financial emergencies, it provides crucial financial support when they occur.

4. **Pay Off Debts**

Debt reduction should be a priority. Clearing your debts frees up more funds for your emergency fund and ensures you're better equipped to handle financial emergencies without the added burden of repayment.

5. **Diversify Your Investments**

Diversifying your investments spreads your risk across different assets, making your financial portfolio more resilient. Short-term, easily accessible investments like money market funds, money market accounts, and high-interest savings accounts are excellent choices for emergency funds. These provide liquidity, allowing you to access your funds quickly if needed.

6. Consult a Financial Planner

If you're uncertain about how to prepare for financial emergencies, consider consulting a certified financial planner. They can assist in creating a customized financial plan that aligns with your needs and risk tolerance. Financial planners can offer guidance on how much to save and where to invest. If you're unsure where to start, you can reach out to organizations like the Foundation for Financial Planning or the Financial Planning Association for free financial advice.

By following these financial preparedness strategies, you can build a robust safety net that will help you weather unexpected financial storms and get back on solid ground. Remember, it's never too late to start preparing for a secure financial future.
[13]

Seeking Assistance in Times of Financial Hardship

In the face of financial emergencies, it's crucial not to hesitate in seeking help. Various organizations and government programs are available to lend support if you find yourself struggling to make ends meet. Here's how you can access assistance when financial challenges arise:

1. Utilize Resources

Organizations like the National Council on Aging provide valuable assistance for elderly and disabled individuals. Their Benefits Checkups Portal can help you identify available benefits and relief programs in your area.

While direct financial aid might not always be an option, these organizations often provide other forms of support, such as meal assistance, transportation services, and more. For instance, the Low-Income Home Energy Assistance Program (LIHEAP) aids eligible low-income households in managing energy costs and home energy-related issues.

---

[13] 4"How to Plan For Financial Emergencies", Students.1fbusa.com, 2021, online, Internet, 26 Sep. 2022. Available: https://students.1fbusa.com/adulthood101/how-to-plan-for-financial-emergencies. 5"Preparing for financial emergencies", GetSmarterAboutMoney.ca, 2022, online, Internet, 21 Sep. 2022. Available:https://www.getsmarteraboutmoney.ca/plan-manage/planning-basics/saving-money/plan-foremergencies/.

2. Access Nutritional Programs

Several programs specifically target low-income seniors to ensure access to nutritious food. The Seniors Farmers Market Nutrition Program (SFMNP) enables them to obtain locally produced fruits and vegetables. Additionally, The Emergency Food Assistance Program (TEFAP) and the Commodity Supplemental Food Program (CSFP) help low-income seniors access essential food resources.

3. Seek Comprehensive Aid

If you require support beyond financial assistance, organizations like Volunteers of America, the National PACE Association, and AmeriCorp offer help in various forms, such as housing aid, medical assistance, and transportation services.

Preparation for Medical Emergencies

A medical emergency can happen suddenly, necessitating immediate medical attention. To ensure you're ready to respond effectively, particularly as you age, it's important to recognize common medical emergencies and have a plan in place. These steps can guide your preparation:

1. Secure Health Insurance

Health insurance plays a pivotal role in safeguarding your financial well-being during a medical crisis. It ensures you're financially prepared for everything from routine doctor's visits to severe emergencies. With health insurance, you can be confident that many medical care expenses are covered, relieving financial concerns during a crisis.

2. Maintain Updated First Aid Kits

Both at home and in your vehicle, having a well-equipped first aid kit is essential. It provides essential supplies and equipment for administering immediate care during a medical emergency. Your first aid kit should include items like bandages, gauze, tape, scissors, tweezers, gloves, antiseptic wipes, soap, and a thermometer.

For more comprehensive preparedness, consider including emergency blankets, splints, CPR masks, and tourniquets. Customize your first aid kit to suit your specific needs or those of your child. For example, if you have asthma, ensure it contains a spare inhaler. Similarly, include an insulin pen or

Epi-Pen if you or your child have diabetes or allergies.

By having these tools and resources on hand, you'll be better prepared to respond to medical emergencies swiftly and effectively. Planning for the unexpected can make all the difference in critical situations.

Become acquainted with the emergency services in your vicinity.[14]

Many individuals are aware of the importance of dialing 911 during emergencies, but what should you do if you find yourself without access to a phone or in an unfamiliar location, unsure of which specific service to contact? In such circumstances, it is highly advisable to acquaint yourself with the emergency services available in your area. This knowledge will empower you to seek assistance when the need arises quickly and efficiently.

Beyond merely recognizing how to reach emergency services, it is also vital to familiarize yourself with the nearest hospital or medical facility. This becomes particularly crucial when you have a child with specific medical requirements, as being aware of which hospitals are best equipped to address their unique needs is of utmost importance. Furthermore, understanding the layout of your local hospital or clinic can prove invaluable in times of crisis, enabling you to swiftly locate various wards and departments when required.

In situations where you are uncertain about whether a situation qualifies as an emergency, it is always wise to err on the side of caution and request assistance. Prioritizing safety over uncertainty is a golden rule to follow.

Additionally, it is highly recommended to carry personal details cards that contain essential information. These cards should include your blood group, allergies, chronic medical conditions, and medication details. In case of an emergency, these cards can save critical time and potentially even save a life. Maintaining a list of close contacts who can be reached during emergencies is equally important. This list should encompass family members, friends, and co-workers who can be quickly contacted in times of crisis. It is essential to ensure that your adult child always has access to such information as well.

---

[14] 6"Healthy Hearts", University of Mississippi Medical Center, 2020, online, Internet, 26 Sep. 2022. Available:https://www.umc.edu/news/Miscellaneous/2020/February/CONSULT%20February%202020/CON022020 A.html. 7"Baby Boomers re-named 'Generation Risk'", Abc.net.au, 2022, online, Internet, 26 Sep. 2022. Available
https://www.abc.net.au/mediawatch/transcripts/1017_generation.pdf.
8"Top 7 Health Concerns for Boomers", Uhhospitals.org, 2016, online, Internet, 26 Sep. 2022. , Available: https://www.uhhospitals.org/Healthy-at-UH/articles/2016/07/top-7-health-concerns-for-boomers.

Furthermore, enrolling in a first aid and CPR course is a proactive step toward being better prepared for medical emergencies. While having a first-aid kit is essential, knowing how to use its contents effectively is equally vital. Enrolling in a first aid and CPR course equips you with the knowledge and skills needed to provide immediate care in case of a medical emergency. These courses are often available at local hospitals, community centers, and through organizations like the Red Cross, making it accessible for individuals to learn these life-saving skills.

Effective emergency preparedness entails a multi-faceted approach encompassing risk assessment, meticulous planning, and proactive readiness. This comprehensive process is crucial for safeguarding both yourself and your child. By dedicating time and effort to diminishing your and your child's exposure to potential risks and implementing measures to mitigate potential hazards, you significantly enhance your ability to confront the unforeseen.

While it's true that it's impossible to foresee or entirely avert every conceivable emergency scenario, your preparedness and planning can serve as a critical differentiator when it comes to handling crisis situations. Keep in mind that in times of emergency, swift and decisive action is imperative. Never hesitate to seek the appropriate form of assistance, as this can be the pivotal factor that determines whether you and your child emerge from the situation unscathed or face disastrous consequences.

To delve further into this, let's explore the key components of effective emergency planning:

1.**Risk Assessment**: Begin by identifying potential risks and vulnerabilities specific to your living environment, family circumstances, and lifestyle. This includes evaluating natural disasters, health emergencies, and safety concerns.

2. **Planning**: Create a comprehensive emergency plan that outlines how you and your child will respond to different types of emergencies. This plan should cover evacuation routes, communication strategies, and essential supplies to have on hand.

3. **Preparedness:** Prepare an emergency kit with essential items such as food, water, medical supplies, and documents. Ensure that everyone in your household knows where to find this kit and understands its contents.

4. **Education**: Educate yourself and your child about the different types of emergencies that could occur and how to respond to them. This includes fire safety, basic first aid, and understanding emergency alerts and warnings.

5. **Communication**: Establish a clear and reliable means of communication with family members, friends, and local authorities during emergencies. Ensure that everyone knows how to contact each other and where to meet if separated.

6. **Community Resources**: Familiarize yourself with local emergency services, such as fire, police, and medical facilities, as well as community resources that can help during emergencies.

7. **Regular Drills**: Conduct emergency drills and exercises with your child to ensure that everyone knows their roles and responsibilities in different emergency scenarios.

By embracing these elements of emergency preparedness, you empower yourself and your child to navigate unexpected situations with confidence and resilience. Remember that in times of crisis, swift action and reaching out for appropriate help can be the linchpin that tips the scales from disaster to safety.

EIGHT

PLANNING THE CONCLUSION OF MY AFFAIRS

"There is a time for birth and a time for passing away."

The events surrounding our birth and the inevitable end of our journey are beyond our control. However, we do possess some agency in orchestrating the affairs that unfold once we depart from this world. While it's an admittedly somber subject, it holds immense significance.

Elderly parents who have adult children with disabilities encounter distinct challenges when it comes to settling their affairs. They bear the responsibility of ensuring that their children will be cared for after their passing, all the while striving to avoid burdening them with the complexities of managing their estate.

This underscores the necessity of formulating comprehensive plans for the conclusion of one's affairs well in advance. To initiate this process, consider the following guidelines:

1. **Secure the Future of Your Financial Interests:**

    - If you own a non-corporate business, you must contemplate its fate after your demise. Ideally, the business should continue to operate, generating income for your family. This can be achieved by designating a willing heir to assume control or by establishing a trust to hold business interests for the benefit of your family.

    - Nonetheless, there may be circumstances where this approach is impractical or undesired. In such cases, your will should delineate how you wish the business to be managed, whether it be sold or dissolved.

- For individuals with retirement accounts, designating a beneficiary is essential. Many retirement accounts bypass the probate process and are directly distributed to the designated beneficiary upon your passing, streamlining the transition of assets.

2. **Safeguard Your Child's Future:**

- Parents of children with disabilities must take extra care in safeguarding their well-being. This includes creating a comprehensive plan that addresses their specific needs, including medical care, housing, and financial support.

- Explore options like special needs trusts, which can ensure your child's financial security without jeopardizing their eligibility for government assistance programs.

3. **Communicate and Document:**

- It is crucial to have open, honest conversations with your family about your intentions and plans. Keeping them informed and engaged in the process can alleviate stress and uncertainty in the future.

- Properly document your wishes, including wills, trusts, and powers of attorney, to ensure that your desires are legally binding and executed as intended.

4. **Seek Professional Guidance:**

- Consult with legal and financial experts who specialize in estate planning. They can provide invaluable insights and help you navigate the complexities of finalizing your affairs.

By taking proactive measures and addressing these considerations, you not only secure your own peace of mind but also provide a stable and secure future for your loved ones, especially those with unique needs. Planning for the conclusion of life's affairs is a responsible and compassionate endeavor, and it is one that should not be delayed.
[15]

---

[15] Ecclesiastes 3:2, New International Version 2Tim Parker, "Do Retirement Accounts Go Through

One crucial aspect to contemplate is whether you wish to allocate funds to charitable causes in your will. This philanthropic gesture not only benefits the chosen charities but can also serve as a strategic means to reduce the tax burden on your estate. Beyond this noble consideration, it's imperative to address various other facets as you plan for the eventualities after your passing.

Managing Debts:

You must also devise a plan for addressing any outstanding debts you may have when you pass away, including credit card debt, mortgages, and car loans. Ideally, you would want these debts to be settled before any assets are transferred to your beneficiaries. However, practical constraints may render this impractical. In such instances, your will should clearly outline how these debts are to be managed. For instance, you might specify that your Executor should liquidate certain assets to settle the outstanding debts. It is essential to ensure that your designated Executor possesses a comprehensive list of your debts and understands how they are to be handled.

Appointment of a Guardian/Conservator:

If you have not yet designated a guardian for your child, it's a matter that warrants your immediate attention. A guardian assumes the critical responsibility of caring for your child after your demise. It is important to note that appointing a guardian is not always obligatory. You should consider this step if your child would otherwise be unable to independently manage their affairs. It's also vital to involve your child in the decision-making process, allowing them a say in selecting their guardian.

A guardian plays a pivotal role in ensuring your child's well-being in your absence, assisting with their day-to-day needs, and facilitating access to essential services. Moreover, the guardian can serve as a protector of your child's financial interests, ensuring that their resources are judiciously managed and safeguarded against potential fraud or exploitation. Knowing that someone is looking out for your child's best interests provides invaluable peace of mind.

The selection of a guardian is a weighty decision, as this individual will shoulder significant responsibilities and make pivotal choices in your child's

---

Probate?", Investopedia, 2021, online, Internet, 26 Sep. 2022. , Available: https://www.investopedia.com/articles/personal-finance/100616/do-retirement accounts-go-through-probate.asp.

life. It is paramount to choose someone whose values align with your own and who you believe will act in your child's best interests. Additionally, the chosen guardian should be well-informed about the responsibilities they will undertake and be willing to fulfill them.

Moreover, you can designate more than one person as a guardian to fulfill different roles in your child's life. For instance, you might appoint one person as the primary guardian and another as the backup guardian. This approach allows for a tailored approach to meet your child's multifaceted needs, whether it concerns their personal care or financial affairs. As you appoint a guardian, it's vital to have in-depth discussions with them, providing comprehensive information about your child, including their medical requirements, preferences, and other essential details.

Craft a Letter of Intent/Instruction:

A letter of intent or instruction is a document that allows you to convey detailed information regarding your child's care. While this document is not legally binding like a will, it serves as a crucial instrument for expressing your wishes to the appointed guardian, other family members, and caregivers. Within this letter, you can encompass an array of information, such as your child's medical needs, educational history, daily routines, favorite activities, dislikes, and any other pertinent details that would facilitate their care.

This letter is also a conduit for articulating your aspirations for your child's future. You can outline your preferences regarding their living arrangements, specific training, or education they should receive, or any unique ambitions you hold for their growth and development. It is also prudent to include details of significant individuals in your child's life and how they can be contacted.

The overarching purpose of this document is to provide a means of communicating your intentions for your child's care. Having this letter in place ensures that everyone involved understands your desires and can act accordingly. While it may not be legally binding, it serves as a guiding beacon, shedding light on how you wish for your child to be cared for and what holds paramount importance to you.

As we delve deeper into the nuances of wills, it's important to recognize their pivotal role in the broader landscape of estate planning.

16

---

[16] 3"The Special Needs Letter of Intent | Special Needs Alliance", Special Needs Alliance, 2009,

Crafting a Will: Securing Your Child's Future

The act of creating a valid will stands as one of the most pivotal and responsible actions you can take to ensure your child's well-being after your passing. The absence of a well-structured will can have detrimental consequences. In the absence of one, your property will be dispersed in accordance with intestacy laws. This poses a significant risk in the case of a child with a disability, as they may inherit a substantial portion of your assets, potentially surpassing income thresholds that render them ineligible for vital benefits. Moreover, probate expenses may consume a substantial portion of your estate.

Perhaps you've already established a will and appointed an executor. However, it's important to note that if you haven't arranged your assets within a trust to safeguard your child's future, you can address this matter either now or through your will.

When composing your will, it's not sufficient merely to specify how your assets should be distributed and which possessions your child should inherit. You must take meticulous care to avoid unintentionally jeopardizing your child's eligibility for government benefits. This underscores the importance of enlisting the expertise of an experienced attorney who specializes in estate planning for individuals with special needs. Such a professional possesses up-to-date knowledge of laws that can influence how you should structure your affairs, thereby enabling you to plan your estate without compromising your child's benefit eligibility.

You can access legal assistance through avenues such as your local chapter of The Arc or organizations like the Special Needs Alliance (SNA), the National Academy of Elder Law Attorneys (NAELA), and The Academy of Special Needs Planners.

Regular Updates and Appointment of Executor:

Your will should undergo regular updates to account for changing circumstances, such as alterations in the value of your assets or potential relocations to different states. Additionally, it is crucial to appoint an executor in your will, granting them easy access to the documents and information necessary to fulfill their responsibilities. The executor holds the crucial role of ensuring your posthumous wishes are executed, underscoring the necessity

---

online, Internet, 19 Sep. 2022. , Available: https://www.specialneedsalliance.org/the-voice/letter-of-intent-4/.

of selecting an individual in whom you have unwavering trust. Furthermore, it is prudent to designate a backup executor in case your primary choice is unable or unwilling to assume the role.

Specific Considerations for Your Will:

Let's delve into specific considerations that your will should encompass:

Disposition of Personal Possessions:

You must contemplate the fate of your personal possessions after your passing, encompassing items like clothing, jewelry, and furniture. Ideally, you would want these items to find appreciative and practical use. You may choose to bequeath your clothes to a charitable organization or bestow your furniture to family members. Alternatively, the proceeds from selling your possessions could be directed toward supporting your child. Furthermore, make provisions for the care of any pets, outlining instructions on who should assume responsibility for their well-being.

Digital Assets:

In our digitally interconnected world, it is paramount to consider the fate of your digital assets, which encompass online accounts, social media profiles, and email accounts. You should determine whether your executor should oversee the deletion of these accounts or make arrangements for their preservation online as a memento, where feasible.

In conclusion, crafting a well-thought-out will represents a pivotal step toward securing your child's future, ensuring their welfare, and managing your legacy responsibly. It is not an endeavor to be undertaken lightly, and professional guidance in this process can be invaluable.

Providing for Your Child's Future:

When you're creating your will, it's not just about distributing your assets; it's also a critical opportunity to ensure the well-being and future of your child. Careful planning is essential to guarantee their living conditions, healthcare, and educational prospects. This comprehensive guide will help you outline and expand upon the essential directives that should be incorporated into your will.

1. **Living Arrangements:**

In your will, you should specify where and with whom you wish your child to reside if you are no longer able to care for them. This might include naming a guardian who will provide a stable and nurturing environment. It's essential to consider the needs and preferences of your child when making this decision.

2. **Healthcare:**

Health-related directives are crucial for your child's well-being. Outline your preferences for medical care, including healthcare providers and any specific medical treatments, should your child require them. You might also want to establish a healthcare proxy or power of attorney to make medical decisions on your child's behalf.

3. **Education and Vocational Therapy:**

Detail your expectations for your child's education and vocational training. Specify any funds or resources set aside for their educational needs, and name individuals responsible for ensuring these resources are used appropriately. If your child has any special needs or requires vocational therapy, make sure your will reflects these considerations.

End-of-Life and Funeral Plans:

Planning for your own end-of-life and funeral arrangements is a thoughtful and considerate act that can relieve your child and other loved ones of significant stress during a difficult time. These plans should not be taken lightly and require careful attention to detail.

1. **Burial or Cremation:**

The first decision to make is whether you prefer burial or cremation. If you choose burial, you will need to purchase a cemetery plot and arrange for a headstone or marker. In the case of cremation, you should select an urn or another suitable container for your ashes.

2. **Funeral Preparations**:

Further, when opting for burial, select a casket, and consider pre-purchasing a vault or grave liner as required by some cemeteries. If you are planning a funeral service, choose a funeral home and make arrangements with their staff. Decide whether you want a visitation, funeral, or memorial service, tailoring the proceedings to your preferences and cultural or religious beliefs.

3. **Writing Your Obituary:**

Taking some time to craft your obituary can be a wonderful way to share your life story with those who know and love you. It's a personal reflection of your life's journey, and by including your wishes in your will, you ensure that your obituary accurately reflects your life and accomplishments.

While planning for end-of-life and funeral arrangements may not be the most pleasant task, it is undeniably crucial. By making these preparations, you guarantee that your final wishes are respected, and you lighten the burden on your loved ones, who won't have to make challenging decisions during their time of grief.

Preparing Your Child for the Transition:

The impending transition for your child, as they face a life without your presence, is undoubtedly a challenging journey. This phase will confront them with the profound loss of a parent and introduce an array of new challenges, forcing them to navigate life without your guidance and support. It is of paramount importance to equip them for this stage of life as thoroughly as possible. Here's an expanded and detailed guide on how to prepare your child:

Honest Communication:
Begin by establishing an open and honest line of communication with your child about your health and prognosis. This candid conversation will help them comprehend the situation and mentally prepare for the potential outcome. Encourage them to ask questions and provide clear, straightforward answers.

Discuss What Comes Next:
In addition to discussing your health, talk to your child about what they can expect after you're gone. Address matters related to living arrangements, guardianship, and any other concerns they may have. Ensuring clarity on these issues can alleviate anxiety.

Continuation of Services:
If your child receives services or support from an organization, make necessary arrangements for these services to continue after your passing.

Ensure that your child's ongoing needs are met.

Quality Time Together:
Make the most of the time you have left by creating meaningful and enjoyable memories with your child. Plan special outings or activities that align with their interests. Consider crafting a bucket list of fun experiences to share with them, ticking off these memorable adventures together.

Mental Preparation:
Support your child's mental well-being by arranging preemptive psychological care. This can help them cope with the emotional impact of your passing and provide essential guidance during this trying time.

Counseling Support:
Ensure that counseling services are available to your child after your death to assist them in navigating the grieving process. Professional support can be invaluable during this emotional journey.

Build Relationships:
Encourage your child to spend time with other family members or friends who can offer emotional support. These relationships will serve as a crucial foundation for them as they adapt to life without you.

Supporting Siblings and Family Members:

Recognize that it's not just your child who will be grieving your loss. Siblings and other family members will also need support. Pay attention to their unique needs and provide assistance where possible. Spend quality time with each of your children individually, ensuring they feel loved and supported.

Define Roles:
Communicate with your family members and define the roles they will play after your passing. Ensure that everyone understands their responsibilities and how they can support one another. This clarity can help alleviate stress during the transition.

Unfinished Business:
Address any unresolved issues with family members. This could involve mending strained relationships, offering apologies for past wrongs, or simply expressing your love and appreciation. These conversations may be challenging but can provide closure and peace for both you and the other individuals involved.

Conclusion:

In your final days, you deserve peace and the assurance that you've addressed the essential aspects of your life. Work diligently to manage your legal and financial affairs and ensure your child is well-prepared for the inevitable transition. Although it is a formidable task, it is also a crucial one. Start your planning now, and with careful execution, ensure that your remaining days are free from worry, surrounded by the love of your child and cherished one.

Nine

FINAL THOUHGTS

Navigating the Next Steps: A New Beginning

As you reach the conclusion of this guide, we want to express our admiration for your dedication and perseverance. You've absorbed a wealth of information, and that, in itself, is a significant accomplishment. Take a moment to reflect on your journey, maybe with a comforting cup of coffee or tea, and allow yourself a well-deserved break. Yes, you read that correctly: you should rest, as your strength will be in high demand ahead.

Why, you may wonder? Well, gathering information is the easy part. The real challenge lies in applying it. It's one thing to understand the importance of self-care and to acknowledge the need for assistance or the release of burdensome properties. However, it's quite another to initiate these changes when you've been accustomed to a particular way of life for so long. We get it; we truly do.

But as you've learned by now, the most worthwhile endeavors are rarely simple, and change is inevitable. It is our duty to attempt to shape change in ways that enhance our lives and those of our loved ones, even when it's a formidable task. Your highest priority should be focused on making these changes a reality.

So, let's get started with the essential tasks. Reach out to special needs attorneys without delay and create a will that outlines your child's guardianship and living arrangements. Manage your finances wisely and explore avenues to increase your financial resources for your child's future care. And amidst all this, remember to maintain an emergency fund that can sustain you and your child for up to six months of daily living.

Don't forget about your own well-being. For now, you are your child's most substantial support. To continue caring for them effectively, prioritize your physical and mental health. Eat well, get sufficient sleep, invest in smart-home technology, allocate time for self-care, prepare for emergencies, and never hesitate to seek assistance when required.

In your journey, remember that help is always available, even when it may not seem so. In addition to local support groups, there are numerous online caregiver forums and communities ready to provide advice and moral support. Organizations like The Arc, Easter Seals, Goodwill Industries, and more can help or guide you to the help you need.

Furthermore, do not overlook the importance of preparing your child for your eventual passing. Have candid conversations with them about what will transpire after your departure and equip them with the tools for independence. Encourage them to make friends, socialize, enroll in vocational programs, and embrace rehabilitation counseling. By doing so, you empower them to rely less on others for their survival.

While we could delve into more details, we trust that you comprehend the essence of what needs to be done. Nevertheless, we want to leave you with three invaluable takeaways:

1. **It's Okay to Feel Overwhelmed:** Feeling overwhelmed is normal and human. When it occurs, do not surrender hope or let negative emotions consume you. Find inspiration in the stories of other caregivers and draw strength from your own past achievements. Remember, you have the strength and determination to see this through.

2. **You Are Not Alone:** You are not alone in this journey. Many others understand your experience and are ready to help, whether it's the organizations mentioned earlier, your support network, or your family and friends. Do not hesitate to seek assistance when needed, as we all require help at times.

3. **Keep an Open Mind:** This guide has introduced you to a world of possibilities, but it only scratches the surface of what you can do. Continue learning, ask questions, and actively seek new information and ideas. Your journey has just begun, and you have many decisions to make and changes to implement. But remember, you can do it, and we'll be here cheering you on until the very end.

THE GUILD OF SEVEN

Acknowledgement

On behalf of The Guild of Seven, we would like to extend our deepest gratitude and heartfelt appreciation to all those who contributed to the creation and realization of this extraordinary book. It is with immense pleasure and honor that we acknowledge the invaluable support and contributions of our colleagues, the dedicated research team, and the inspiring testimonies from the families involved.

To our colleagues, we extend our sincerest thanks for their unwavering support, collaboration, and expertise throughout this remarkable journey. Their dedication and enthusiasm have been instrumental in shaping the vision and content of this book. Their insightful discussions, constructive feedback, and tireless efforts have truly enriched its narrative, making it a significant contribution to the field.

We would also like to express our profound gratitude to the exceptional research team that tirelessly delved into the depths of knowledge and uncovered hidden gems to illuminate the pages of this work. Their commitment to thoroughness, meticulousness, and accuracy has ensured that this book stands as a beacon of reliable information, ready to enlighten readers for generations to come.

Our deepest appreciation extends to the courageous families who entrusted us with their personal testimonies, enabling us to weave together a tapestry of human experiences and emotions. Their openness, vulnerability, and willingness to share their stories have breathed life into these pages, making this book a testament to the resilience and strength of the human spirit.

Furthermore, we would like to express our gratitude to the countless individuals who have supported us behind the scenes, offering encouragement, understanding, and patience during the demanding process of bringing this book to fruition. Their unwavering belief in our mission and their unwavering support have been a source of motivation and inspiration.

Lastly, we would like to extend our heartfelt thanks to the readers who have embraced this book. It is your curiosity, engagement, and appreciation that drive us to continue our pursuit of knowledge and understanding.

This book stands as a collective achievement, made possible through the collaboration, dedication, and commitment of all those involved. We are humbled and grateful to have had the opportunity to work with such remarkable individuals and to bring this labor of love into the world.

With sincere appreciation,

The Guild of Seven

Guild of Seven

The members of Guild of Seven are specialists in their fields who are committed to helping others via their work. Led by the founder Elizabeth O'Carroll MRC, M.Ed., Guild of Seven's mission to equip and educate seniors who are caring for adult disabled children on how to provide for themselves and their offspring in their later years and after their passing.

Our publications offer a wide range of views and information since each member of our team contributes their own viewpoint and area of expertise to the table. We appreciate that every household is on a different path, and we do our best to offer advice that is accessible, practical, and personally relevant.

Here at Guild of Seven, we know that working together can produce amazing results. Our publications provide insight with up-to-date answers to life's common and unique hurdles by bringing together a team of dedicated professionals and research specialists.

BIBLIOGRAPHY

Web Pages

Adult Foster Care: How It Works, Financial Assistance & Payment Options, Payingforseniorcare.com, 2020, online, Internet, 16 Sep. 2022. , Available: https://www.payingforseniorcare.com/adult-foster-care.

"Facts & Figures", Ahcancal.org, 2022, online, Internet, 21 Sep. 2022. , Available: https://www.ahcancal.org/Assisted-Living/Facts-and-Figures/Pages/default.aspx.

"Fall prevention: Simple tips to prevent falls", Mayo Clinic, 2022, online, Internet, 26 Sep. 2022. , Available: https://www.mayoclinic.org/healthy-lifestyle/healthy-aging/in-depth/fall-prevention/art-20047358

"Healthy Hearts", University of Mississippi Medical Center, 2020, online, Internet, 26 Sep. 2022. , Available:https://www.umc.edu/news/Miscellaneous/2020/February/CONSULT%20February%202020/CON022020A.html.

"How to Plan For Financial Emergencies", Students.1fbusa.com, 2021, online, Internet, 26 Sep. 2022. , Available: https://students.1fbusa.com/adulthood101/how-to-plan-for-financial-emergencies

"Top 7 Health Concerns for Boomers", Uhhospitals.org, 2016, online, Internet, 26 Sep. 2022. , Available: https://www.uhhospitals.org/Healthy-at-UH/articles/2016/07/top-7-health-concerns-for-boomers

Amanda Lambert, "5 Main Types of Assisted Living Options for Young Adults | Cake Blog", Joincake.com, 2022, online, Internet, 15 Sep. 2022. , Available:https://www.joincake.com/blog/assisted-living-for-youngadults/

Anna Medaris Miller and Lisa Esposito, "8 Factors to Consider When Choosing an Assisted Living Facility", US News, 2022, online, Internet, 20 Sep. 2022. , Available: https://health.usnews.com/best-assisted-living/articles/6-factors-to-consider-when-choosing-an-assisted-living-facility#events.

Charlotte Gerber, "How to Choose a Group Home for a Disabled Loved One", Verywell Health, 2022, online, Internet, 21 Sep. 2022. , Available: https://www.verywellhealth.com/group-homes-for-the-disabled1094358.

Charlotte Gerber, "How to Choose a Group Home for a Disabled Loved One", Verywell Health, 2020, online, Internet, 21 Sep. 2022. , Available: https://www.verywellhealth.com/group-homes-for-the-disabled1094358.

Eva Frederick, "What happens to our online lives after we die?", Science.org, 2020, online, Internet, 27 Sep. 2022. , Available: https://www.science.org/content/article/what-happens-our-online-lives-after-we die.

Gates, R., n.d. What are Income Based Clinics - HealthCore Clinic. [online] HealthCore Clinic. Available at: <https://healthcoreclinic.org/2020/10/03/what-are-income-based-clinics> [Accessed 7 September 2022]

Maeve Duggan, "What happens to your digital life after death?", Pew Research Center, 2013, online, Internet, 27 Sep. 2022. , Available: https://www.pewresearch.org/fact-tank/2013/12/02/what-happens-toyour-digital-life-after-death/.

Preparing for financial emergencies", GetSmarterAboutMoney.ca, 2022, online, Internet, 21 Sep. 2022. , Available:https://www.getsmarteraboutmoney.ca/plan-manage/planning-basics/saving-money/plan-foremergencies/

Tim Parker, "Do Retirement Accounts Go Through Probate?", Investopedia, 2021, online, Internet, 26 Sep. 2022. , Available: https://www.investopedia.com/articles/personal-finance/100616/do-retirement-accounts-go-through-probate.asp.

UK Care Guide. 2022. ADVANTAGES & DISADVANTAGES OF LIVE IN CARE 2022 - What are they?. [online] Available at: <https://ukcareguide.co.uk/main-advantages-disadvantages-live-care/> [Accessed 7 September 2022]

Journals

Curtis S. Florence et al., "Medical Costs of Fatal and Nonfatal Falls in Older Adults", Journal of the American Geriatrics Society 66.4 (2018): 693-698, online, Internet, 16 Sep. 2022. , Available: https://www.ncbi.nlm.nih.gov/pmc/articles/PMC6089380/#R1

Donna Dosman and Norah Keating, "Cheaper for Whom? Costs Experienced by Formal Caregivers in Adult Family Living Programs", Journal of Aging & Social Policy 17.2 (2005): 67-83, online, Internet, 21 Sep. 2022

J A Stevens et al., "The costs of fatal and non-fatal falls among older adults", Injury Prevention 12.5 (2006): 290-295, online, Internet, 22 Sep. 2022. , Available: https://www.ncbi.nlm.nih.gov/pmc/articles/PMC2563445/.

J. Reinardy and R. A. Kane, "Choosing an Adult Foster Home or a Nursing Home: Residents' Perceptions about Decision Making and Control", Social Work 44.6 (1999): 571-585.

O'Dwyer, S., Janssens, A., Sansom, A., Biddle, L., Mars, B., Slater, T., Moran, P., Stallard, P., Melluish, J., Reakes, L., Walker, A., Andrewartha, C. and Hastings, R., 2021. Suicidality in family caregivers of people with long-term illnesses and disabilities: A scoping review. Comprehensive Psychiatry, 110, p.152261.

Online PDFs

"The Special Needs Letter of Intent | Special Needs Alliance", Special Needs Alliance, 2009, online, Internet, 19 Sep. 2022. , Available: https://www.specialneedsalliance.org/the-voice/letter-of-intent-4/

Sharon Davis, A Family Handbook on Future Planning, ebook (The Arc of the United States and the Rehabilitation Research and Training Center (RRTC) on Aging with Developmental Disabilities, 2003), online, Internet, 25 Sep. 2022. , Available: https://www.wrightslaw.com/info/future.planning.arc.pdf.

With Open Arms. Ebook. Easter Seals, and The National Endowment For Financial Education, 2002. Online. Internet. 26 Sep. 2022. . Available:https://secure.easterseals.com/site/DocServer/Easter_Seals_ _With_Open_Arms.doc?docID=1341.

Who.int, 2022, online, Internet, 18 Sep. 2022. , Available: https://www.who.int/docs/default source/documents/disability/covid-19-disability-briefing.pdf.

Independentfutures.com, 2014, online, Internet, 21 Sep. 2022. , Available: https://independentfutures.com/wp-content/uploads/2018/06/EnglishHousingGuide-min.pdf. Ecclesiastes 3:2, New International Versio

www.ingramcontent.com/pod-product-compliance
Lightning Source LLC
Chambersburg PA
CBHW070620050426
42450CB00011B/3092